AF492595

HONEY, CHECK IT!

"Lauren White is the friend you wish lived next door. She is a porch friend. A long, lazy-afternoon-chat friend. The friend you can trust to be honest but kind, sassy but generous, willing to stand with you both through nights that weigh heavy with grief and on the ones that are clear and studded with stars and possibility. Lauren is that kind of friend, and she has written a book for all of us. *Honey, Check It!* is a beautiful call to remember what's true in all seasons: that we are beloved by the God who made us, that this story we are living isn't over yet, that we can learn to watch for God's goodness in the most unlikely places, and that we do all of these things better when we link arms. I loved this book."

—Kimberly Stuart, author of *Star for Jesus*
(And Other Jobs I Quit)

"Reading Lauren's book, *Honey, Check It!*, felt like having coffee every morning with a wise and Godly friend. Even though Jesus himself told us we would have trouble in this world, there is still a tendency for us to be shocked and unequipped when it comes our way. Lauren helps teach us how to hold joy and pain together by sharing her heart-wrenching story of loss upon loss upon loss. If you have found yourself unprepared for great sorrow in the past, do yourself a favor and read this book! It will give you invaluable tools to keep moving forward and glorifying God when the going gets tough. For a new perspective of our 'everywhere God', look no further than *Honey, Check It!* It's the perfect mix of humor, vulnerability, and truth."

—Shelley Breen, Point of Grace

"This book is a beautiful encouragement for all of us, a reminder to *refocus* our lens of life. It helps us shift our perspective to see God *with us*—in *all* parts of our stories . . . the good, the hard, and the in-between."

—Meshali Mitchell, acclaimed photographer, visual storyteller,
faith-based speaker, and podcaster

"There are two types of people: People who have been through seasons of asking God 'Why?' and people who are going to go through seasons of asking God 'Why?' Lauren's book applies to both types! Life can be brutal, and the Bible can be confusing, but *Honey, Check It!* has a masterful, yet irresistible way of applying God's truths in the seasons of 'Why?' Bless yourself and everyone around you by taking in all that this gem has to offer!"

—Dr. T. Kale Gober, Vice President of Advancement, Grand Canyon University

"Honey, Check It! is a resource I will share with clients who are walking through grief and loss. Lauren White shares her personal experiences with authenticity while pointing her readers to Christ and the hope found in Him. Filled with stories from her own life and wisdom she's learned along the way, Lauren provides us with practical steps to broaden our perspective of God's presence during difficult seasons of life. If you need some encouragement in your life, this is just the book for you. It's full of vulnerable stories that highlight the nearness of God."

—Aamie Mason, Living Well Professional Counseling, LPC

"Not being a big coffee drinker, I've never been to a coffee gathering where neuroplasticity was discussed. Thank you, Lauren, not only for the excellent explanation, but also (more importantly) for the reminder that we need some spiritual neuroplasticity to rewire our minds and hearts. Walking through this compelling memoir has been an excellent reminder of our constant need for a proper focus on our awesome God. At the completion of each chapter, whether painful or joyful, Lauren always puts the focus on the perfect purpose of God and calls for our proper response: remember the Lord, who has always been with us and always will be with us, here, there, and everywhere. Lauren, thanks for the challenge to the soul work of spiritual neuroplasticity."

—Dave Hughey, lead pastor of Geyer Springs First Baptist Church, friend, and husband to Cita

HONEY, CHECK IT!

Enhancing our Perspective with a
Here, There, Everywhere God

L. Y. White

Honey, Check It! Enhancing our Perspective with a Here, There, Everywhere God

© 2024 by L. Y. White.
Paperback Edition

All rights reserved. No portion of this book may be reproduced, stored in a retrieval system, or transmitted in any form or by any means—electronic, mechanical, photocopy, recording, scanning, or other—except for brief quotations in critical reviews or articles, without the prior written permission of the publisher.

Published in Little Rock, Arkansas, by DL Flair, LLC.

Scripture verses marked CSB are from The Christian Standard Bible. Copyright © 2017 by Holman Bible Publishers. Used by permission. Christian Standard Bible®, and CSB® are federally registered trademarks of Holman Bible Publishers, all rights reserved.
Scripture verses marked ESV are from The Holy Bible, English Standard Version. ESV® Text Edition: 2016. Copyright © 2001 by Crossway Bibles, a publishing ministry of Good News Publishers.

Editor: Jamie Chavez
Typesetter: Paul Salvette
Book Cover Design: ebooklaunch.com
Author Photo: Ashley Milam Photography

ISBN 979-8-9896710-1-4 (Print Paperback)

Library of Congress Cataloging-in-Publication Data
2024903847
Printed in the United States of America

*For my Austin, Emmie, Atalie, and Julianna . . . forever my
For-You-I-Wills.*

*For my momma and daddy who will never get to read this book
on this side of heaven . . . this story for God's glory is
your legacy.*

Table of Contents

Foreword

WHEN I WAS GROWING UP, I LEARNED THAT WHEN I PLAYED by the rules my parents would give me encouragement and affirmation and my small heart soared when they did. When I would do things that displeased my parents, it felt like they would physically and emotionally turn their backs on me. This was the genesis of the idea planted in my young mind that love was something that could be either given or withdrawn as a tool for controlling my behaviors. Stated differently, love was a weapon that could be taken away as quickly as it was given and hence wasn't something that could be trusted.

We all are, to a greater or lesser degree, predisposed to be the sum of all the experiences and interactions we have had, both good and bad. What can change this is developing a new perspective on who we are and what our lives' purpose is. My good friend Lauren has written a book which invites you into the chaos, not to see the vacuum it creates, but the joy it can become filled with. As you turn these pages you will smell the cookies in the oven as you feel like you are talking to an old friend as Lauren invites you into her delightful and very real world. She does not catastrophize nor minimize the lessons she has learned in life. Instead, she reminds us that nothing is wasted: not our pain and confusion, and certainly not our mistakes.

Life is a whole lot of ambiguity followed by an eternity of certainty. Lauren hopes you will cast off the dock line, unfurl your sails and set out on an adventure with her. She wants you to know you are loved; that God is nuts about you and the idea of spending an eternity together is too short for Him. Through the lens of a dedicated wife, mother, and a professional nurse, Lauren invites us to look at why we do what we do and borrows science, psychology, and other disciplines to point us toward greater truths for our lives.

You are about to experience a life change. Buckle up, settle in, and prepare to experience Lauren's unique bedside manner in these pages.

Bob Goff,
Chief Balloon Inflator and author of
four *New York Times* best-selling books

Introduction

Our Perspective Is Everything

"**C**OME ON, MOMMA, LET'S GO!"

I'm usually a road runner speed walker. Totally the crazy lady that people see as they drive down the road and think, *Let's be sure to stay out of her walking lane so we don't get plowed over* or *What kind of caffeine does she drink?* (Sidenote: I don't drink caffeine because apparently God piggybacked it onto my DNA. Excess stimulant would only cause daily stumbling for my hyped-up self). But on this morning, as I was trailing behind our daughters on the road headed toward my momma's house, my speed button was locked. I stood paused in the middle of the black asphalt as my heart fluttered and I took a long breath. You see, walking like three ducks in a row, my children were unknowingly enlightening my heart and sharpening my perspective as they traveled to see their Yaya.

Our oldest daughter, Emmie, age seven, was first in line. She stopped for a minute to pace a small area as she assessed a critter bug that was in between the sidewalk and the neighbors' luscious green grass. Our Emmie is always taking in her surroundings and being watchful of anything new. **Adventurous** was the neon light I saw shining over her swaying ponytail.

Following close behind, never to be outdone by her one-minute-older twin sister, was our Atalie, who had endured an insanely traumatic leg injury a short month prior to that day. The G-rated version is that she sliced her leg open on a razor-sharp brick wall that landed us in the emergency room for hours and our sweet girl in a straight leg brace for several weeks. This morning, she was walking with her cane (a significant upgrade from her walker). Gimping like a peg leg pirate, Atalie had a smile on her face and determination in her eyes, as she was eager to get down to her Yaya's house for some morning fun. **Slightly Broken but Overcoming** was the neon light I envisioned flashing above her.

The caboose of this duck line was Julianna, our youngest and spiciest daughter. Sister glided down the street in a ballet costume that was two sizes too big, but she insisted it was the perfect match for her tennis shoes and floral ribbon scrunchie. This princess walks with her pinkies out at all times because, well, what other hand position is appropriate for royalty? **Whimsical** was the neon light flickering over her tiny majesty.

As I was catching a deep breath and seeing all these flashing signs over my daughters, I became over-whelmed with the idea that in a single day or season of our lives, the spotlights on our life's stage can beam through lenses of many emotions and states-of-being. It was the vast difference of three little girls journeying to their grandmother's house that sealed the envelope of this life lesson for me. Sometimes our feelings are joyful and full of whimsy. Some days our pulse is for learning and adventure. Other days, we feel beat down to a pulp by the hurts of financial strain, relationship fallout, and self-doubt. But even in the flow of happy or hard, we keep moving forward because life keeps happening. The sun continues to come up each day and the date on the calendar turns. Ah, *c'est la vie.*

Yet often I have found myself irritated by the resuming of a world in motion when my personal life feels frozen in heartache or struggle. Anyone with me on that?

Here's what I think: *We can't plan our circumstances, but we can plan our perspective on how we live through those circumstances.*

Perspective.

This is the overarching neon sign that I want us to home in on as we travel through this book together. Our perspective on daily happenings can sway if we're not deliberately checking it in each situation.

From a decade of complex lessons that (in my opinion) seemed to come too early on my life's timeline, I (and my family) have had to deal with an array of trouble and hard lessons: loss of babies and loved ones, reality checks of my own tunnel-visioned perspective, and more. To be frank, I've wrestled with fully believing and standing on the goodness of the God who created us. To find comfort and calm in the chaos of my life events, I had to do some deep analyzing of my heart, thought processing, and daily intentions.

If faith is your north star, then come on, let's keep traveling down this perspective road together. If your north star is something else, don't jump ship. Let's lock arms together. If you were to walk into my house today, you would find an oversized canvas that was masterfully crafted by a dear family friend hanging beside our whitewashed dining table. In the corner of this artwork, you will read three words in gold paint. "There you are." Our family's heartbeat is for others to always know that they are seen by us. We are excited to see others come into our home. Within the binding of this book is my invitation just for you to come and sit at our dining room table. Please make sure to soak in those three words, *There you are*, as you sit down.

I see you. And I'm pumped that you're joining me on this adventure. Friend, to anyone who has ever felt the emotions of happiness or somberness, *you are welcome in this space*. And I think that if you give this God-infused story a listen, you'll find that you are never alone in your circumstances.

It took me years to sift and sort through all my life's unfolding. I viewed each circumstance through many lenses. Secular, self-sufficient, and scattered. But for me, it all came back to one shining star—there was no way for me personally to fix the hurtful parts of my story. Yet I kept hearing a whisper to *remember* that the God who is in all my life's victories and delights is the same God in the ouch and unfun parts too. The reason God stays with you and me through it *all* is because of His mind-blowing adoration and love for us. We'll dive into more specifics on that big statement later. But for now, I need you to hear and absorb these truths. We are chosen by God, made in His image, and we *are* loved and forgiven.

Once I fully absorbed whose I was and what God created me to be—chosen, loved, forgiven, the light of the world, created in the image of Him, redeemed, and strong—my lens on life became 20/20. Please don't hear me say that I'm forever healed and life from now on will be hunky-dory, without heartache or failures. I have blood pumping through my veins and breath in my lungs, therefore, I'm a living human being who is unable to find perfection. Period.

But friends, those characteristics of who I am in Christ aren't just descriptions of me. They belong to every single one of us—whether we accept it or not. If you just rolled your eyes or squirmed in your seat due to that unsettled feeling as you thought of applying words like *chosen, loved, forgiven, light of the world*, and *made in God's image* to yourself, my prayer is that by the end of this book, you will fully claim who God says you are. (Your girl, here, is a master eye-roller, hand on the hip, and pursed-lip, attitude-throwing sister. I've been in your doubting shoes. And I stood there tall in all my sass and pride. But I had a vision checkup that squashed that sass and pride.)

You are chosen.

You are loved.

You are forgiven.

You are the light of the world.

You are 100 percent created in the image of a remarkable God.

You are redeemed.

And, honey, *you are* strong.

Despite my humanness, the lens I see life through today is completely different than my lens of a decade ago. When my heart perspective changed from the inside out, so did my eyeball perspective. As I intentionally searched for God in all of life's circumstances, I have found and remembered Him to be there in the ups and the downs. Isn't it easy for us to ask, "Where are you, God?" when life stinks and doesn't go the way we'd like? The blame game is easy for believers and nonbelievers. Remembering God when life is peachy keen isn't always the extra step that we want to take. The gratitude game is much trickier and time-consuming to play. Once we acknowledge that God is with us on all accounts, our life's lens—our perspective—becomes reframed.

This shift of perspective isn't a quick-fix pill to swallow, it's a lifestyle change and will take daily intentionality.

Consider this scenario. Body armor for our police force isn't light. But if the valiant men and women who protect our communities don't suit up, they are vulnerable to worldly dangers. The lens that we view life through can be vulnerable to a secular perspective if we don't suit up each day with a biblical perspective. Embracing this lens on life isn't always the easy and feel-good route, but I've tried non-biblical perspectives and they leave me repeatedly beat down with a hopeless conclusion.

One morning I was sitting in a sauna sweating bullets as I listened to a podcast. I wanted all the toxins inside my body to continue seeping out, but the wisdom that I heard from guest Katy Faust on the Mama Bear Apologetics[1] podcast was something I wanted to fully absorb and retain. Katy is the founder and president of Them Before Us, a global movement defending children's right to their mothers and fathers. On this day's episode, Katy was dialing in on the impact of marriage and divorce on children. She said, "You become what you behold . . . and culture is forcing us to behold all manners of dysfunction." This idea deeply resonated with my heart. I felt that those words were applicable in so many realms of our lives, not just in the arena of marriage and divorce. The idea that we become what we see and observe is so profound. You don't have to be a Christian to know that what we see happening around us in this world is nuts. So we circle back to having a planned perspective for all of life. *What do we choose to prioritize in our day to day? What and whom are we beholding?* When our perspective is one of biblical truth and knowing who we are, then we find life and freedom in Jesus's love.

The rolling out of three different states of emotions from my daughters walking in the same moment of time has reframed my perspective forever. We are each in a driver's seat for keeping our perspective in check. It is our choice to remember and find the unchanging and everpresent God who has scripted our lives. God's word tells us in Proverbs 8:35, "For whoever finds me finds life and obtains favor from the LORD" (ESV). I don't know about you but I crave life every day. A life full of purpose, kindness, and fun. And even though life isn't guarenteed to be kind and fun every day, we can still seek out the God who is fully present and gives us purpose in our every day. "I love those who love me, and those who seek me diligently find me" (v. 17 ESV). These hope-filled words are from Proverbs chapter 8, as well. It doesn't say "good luck finding me" as if we're playing the lengthiest and most intense game of hide-and-seek with God. No. It says those who seek me diligently *find me*.

We're going to work together on suiting up in the only daily perspective that I've found to keep me sane and joyfilled despite my heartaches and crazy in life. A biblical perspective.

God is with us in the here and now.

God was with us in the days gone by.

And God is everywhere around us as we move into the future.

PART 1

Preamble

It's Science, Y'all

I'M *A SERVANT AND CHEERLEADER BY HEART, BUT A NURSE* by trade. After watching the endless servanthood of my momma all of my growing-up years, I knew that I wanted to be a full-time, stay at home mom when I grew up. Of course, in my adolescent years I understood anatomy and physiology to some extent and realized that I might need to have a backup career until I found my prince or felt led to adopt and start a family—so nursing it was. The thought of going to work every day and being paid to care for patients through words and action seemed like a dream. I had the joy of serving patients in the pediatric and adult population for five years before our twin princesses made their debut in 2014.

With that said, I'm utterly intrigued by the human body and its complexities. From the noises and secretions it makes (marriage and motherhood has only intensified my awareness of this phenomena), to the process of what happens after eating a hamburger one day and how our body uses the good stuff and "passes" the waste the next day, all of it totally fascinates me.

Thanks to scientists and their passion for finding clarity in the functioning of the human body, I've been able to gain a better understanding and perspective for what and why certain thoughts and physical symptoms overtake me at upsetting times. Wise therapists have further explained to me the way our brains, hearts, and bodies work with one another. Remember, we get to choose our perspective on daily living. After a lot of flops, I've learned how critical it is to make sure the voices we give the microphone to in our lives are sound. Just because somebody has a lot of letters behind their name doesn't mean that their heart perspective is sound. It means they're really good at school. Let's not hand over our microphone to just anyone.

As a now, self-aware worrier, I've tuned in to the voices of many therapists and leaders whom I have found to be truth giving and followers of Jesus. These are the people I'm handing my microphone to. In my researching, self-reflecting, and listening to wise counsel, I've discovered that somewhere between the age of one and twenty-five, I was crowned with the title of Miss Anxiety.

Sissy Goff is a brilliant, licensed professional counselor who is furthering God's kingdom alongside her pet therapist, Lucy, in a little yellow house in Nashville, Tennessee. Sissy has tremendously helped me to better understand my battles with worry and anxiety.

For starters, she brought clarity to some key words that I've needed a better grasp on.[2] Fear is something that we're afraid *of* and it's specifically tied to a certain object or situation. Rest assured that this emotion is completely normal and helps us when we're faced with life-threatening situations.

Worry, however, is a bigger fish to fry. We worry *about* situations that may or may not have occurred. This worry-fish can lead to anxiety, which causes our worried thoughts or images to get stuck like a single-loop roller coaster.

That's the alarm. If you've noticed that you're stuck on a one-loop roller coaster that holds you captive to unhelpful ways in life, then hear this: "Ladies and gentlemen, this ride is permanently shut down. Please exit *now*." In this world where we can become stuck and sedated with busyness and complacency, we must wake up to awareness and action.

We will begin by unpacking some facts about the folded organ in our head that is capable of remarkable functioning—our brains.

If you're like me, you might just find your shoulders relaxing and a personal narrative of "there's just something weird about me" fading away as we learn about our brain's capabilities. It might even change your perspective.

At your latest coffee gathering, did you unpack *brain neuroplasticity*? Yeah, I didn't either. And my coffee gatherings usually look like my mom-wagon curbing the pavement of Starbucks' drive-thru line as my daughters giggle and put in orders for cake pops from the back seats. Neuroplasticity isn't on my radar then, but it is now.

Our brains have the ability to rewire themselves, which is what neuroplasticity refers to. What we learn today—like the lyrics to a new song or the location of a restaurant—causes our brains to physically change. Neurons function as little information messengers throughout our brains. The messages are sent either chemically or electrically and the connections between the neurons are constantly reshaping. This explains how we're *literally* not the same people that we were yesterday because our brain has worked tirelessly throughout the day to decipher and reroute all sorts of information, which has paved a new pathway. Though humans don't come fully preprogrammed, we are able to adapt to different environments and circumstances through the firing of neurons that are trying to learn from their new settings and situations. As neuroscientist David Eagleman said, "Brains never reach an end point. We spend our lives blossoming toward something, even as the target moves."[3]

That all sounds pretty cool, right?

So what happens if someone has a stroke or must have a part of their brain removed due to illness or trauma? Thankfully, the way God created humans as live-wired rather than hard-wired allows us to hold on to hope for regaining some if not all function after medically trying events.

There once was a boy named Matthew who was diagnosed with a rare and chronic brain disease. He suffered several seizures each day, and his doctor recommended a hemispherectomy—surgically removing an entire half of the brain. Matthew's parents chose the surgical treatment route. Can you even imagine the bravery it took for his parents to choose such a risky procedure and open-ended outcome for their son?

Though incontinent and unable to walk or speak following the surgery, three months postoperatively and post-therapy, Matthew was developmentally appropriate. Isn't that remarkable? He worked through therapies where he relearned how to understand and speak words. Years later, Matthew did walk with a slight limp and was unable to use his right hand well. Yet despite those physical observations, Matthew's mother said that people wouldn't have the slightest clue that he was missing half of his brain.

Neuroplasticity was the key factor that drove Matthew's body to refunctioning. As Dr. Eagleman notes about Matthew's story, "The blueprints of his nervous system adjusted themselves to occupy a smaller piece of real estate—encompassing the fullness of life with half the machinery. You couldn't slice out half the electronics from your smartphone and hope to still make a call, because hardware is fragile. Liveware (the essence of our brains) endures."[4]

Just as physical therapy and daily interactions can literally change our physical minds, so can the words and stories that we tell ourselves.

Ding! Ding! Ding! Did you get that? This is information we can use.

This idea is referred to as *self-directed neuroplasticity.* We can rewire our brains by rewriting our daily narratives. Psychiatrist Dr. Joseph A. Annibali, also known as "the brain whisperer" says, "Brain scans show evidence of brain alterations that resemble the changes brought about by medication in people who undertake cognitive behavior therapy (CBT), which is simply a structured version that teaches retelling of your stories. Other brain scan research also supports this claim of self-directed neuroplasticity from rewriting your story. For example, the work of Jeffrey Schwartz, M.D., at UCLA demonstrates brain changes from mindfulness-based interventions for obsessive-compulsive disorder (OCD). Schwartz's mindfulness approach is close to retelling your story. *The key point is that changing how you talk to yourself, changing what you say to yourself, how you tell yourself stories, changes your brain.*"[5] (Emphasis mine.)

Ding! Ding! Ding (again)! Highlight that last sentence because it is rich in truth and scientific evidence.

The words that we use to talk to ourselves within our heads are crucial to how our brains continue to form. If our perspective is one of a biblical worldview—chasing after Jesus and bringing God glory—then the words we rattle off in response to happy or hard situations are going to make our lives better.

Of course, we're human, and we will have seasons when our thoughts are potholes and our words are debris on our life-road, but we're driving the car. As soon as we acknowledge the unwholesome and junky thoughts within, we can hit the brakes, dodge the mess, or altogether detour.

We have hope to move through this life without feeling horrible when things don't go the way we would have liked. First and foremost, because Jesus Christ paid for our gift of hope when He was crucified on the cross.

Secondly, through the hope in our bodies' ability to heal and rewire—because it was crafted by God, the ultimate Healer and Creator.

At the end of each chapter, you will find a couple of questions and affirmations to help guide you into further self-directed neuroplasticity. Look at us being all suave in the science world.

You will recognize this section when you see this heading: **Check It**. We're going to intentionally pause between chapters to check our specs, if you will. We'll focus on our perspective of details and ideas in the moment. Take some time to think through the questions. Dig into God's word even further when it's hard to reach a launching or landing pad for an answer. Call a friend and go walk laps in your driveway together as you formulate thoughts. I haven't a doubt in my mind that the Holy Spirit will meet you wherever you are seeking Him.

Following the questions will be an affirmation that will be repeated at the end of each chapter. This is where we get to work on the self-directed neuroplasticity. By the end of the book, you'll know the affirmation lines better than any actress in Hollywood knows her script. It includes a reference to Psalm 77:1–14, so let's talk about that.

Psalm 77

 CRY ALOUD TO GOD, ALOUD TO GOD, AND HE WILL HEAR me. In the day of my trouble I seek the Lord; in the night my hand is stretched out without wearying; my soul refuses to be comforted. When I remember God, I moan; when I meditate, my spirit faints. *Selah.* You hold my eyelids open; I am so troubled that I cannot speak. I consider the days of old, the years long ago. I said, "Let me remember my song in the night; let me meditate in my heart." Then my spirit made a diligent search: 'Will the Lord spurn forever, and never again be favorable? Has his steadfast love forever ceased? Are his promises at an end for all time? Has God forgotten to be gracious? Has he in anger shut up his compassion?' *Selah.* Then I said, 'I will appeal to this, to the years of the right hand of the Most High.' I will remember the deeds of the LORD; yes, I will remember your wonders of old. I will ponder all your work, and meditate on your mighty deeds. Your way, O God, is holy. What god is great like our God? You are the God who works wonders..." (Psalm 77:1–14 ESV).

It is thought, by the way, that *selah* means "stop and listen." Word to the wise, right?

From some voluntary and involuntary heart work, my husband, Austin, and I have found these verses to be a genuine treasure and guiding star in our self-directed neuroplasticity. When we jump with joy, scream in brokenness, and burn with anger from misunderstandings, these verses are the repeat directions we encode into our thoughts and prayers.

In a condensed and bulleted rendition, it looks something like this.

- Cry out to God.
- Seek the Lord.
- *Remember* God.
- Feel all the feels (this can include questioning).
- *Remember* the days gone by and meditate in your heart.
- Proclaim and believe in the God who has reigned in the happy and hard.

These fourteen verses are life-sustaining to our family. To hear that we can lament and cry out to God in the times of hurt supplies me oxygen in my dreaded, breath-holding moments. So often, society's conventions make us conceal our real emotions and guilt-trip us into putting on our big-people undies to get over whatever our issue is. Yet our loving, heavenly Father nudges us to *remember* the days of old—to remember His kindness and steadfast, manifesting presence. When we feel so troubled that we can't form words or keep our eyelids open from the exhaustion and turmoil of our circumstances, we get to feel all the emotions of our situations, but we should quickly follow them and rebuke them with the memories of God's presence in *all* times.

Prayer, fasting, worship, and Sabbath are all spiritual disciplines that often get the spotlight. But what about *remember*? This eight-letter word is a powerful practice, yet is easily forgotten.

In the book of Joshua, twelve stones serve as symbols of God's might. For generations to come, the Israelites were to tell their children the stones were from the Jordan River that God dried up to allow the Israelites safe passage across. These stones were visuals of God's presence and promises fulfilled.

We may not save every ripped-off car bumper from a wreck or intravenous bag from a hospital stay, but the act of our remembering God's presence can infuse our self-directed neuroplasticity with grace.

Often, people mean well when they say, "Don't look behind you, just push forward." Yes, we shouldn't dwell on all that has gone wrong in the past, but there are times that in order for us to move forward with hope in life, we need to look back and reflect on God's presence from our past.

If it weren't important to look behind us, rearview mirrors would be removed from all vehicle assembly lines. Yet they're not. Actually, production is zooming in even closer on what's behind. Backup cameras are all the rage—and obviously, a safety bonus. How about the mainstream automobile lines that put "rear-seat occupant alerts" as part of all standard packages these days? Hm.

Sounds like it's a big deal to know what's behind us, right?

This act of spiritual discipline, remembering, is a crucial practice that can help us to thrive in this world. To lament and cry out from a heart of doubt or shaky faith can be hard when you would rather be a happy-go-lucky kind of gal. We don't want to sit and stew on the negative, *but* it's OK to go there. It's OK to acknowledge and speak of hardships. Even Jesus wept and asked questions in His lifetime. Y'all, that's God in the flesh giving us permission and freedom to feel. *Joy* and *pain* coexist and it's OK to put those two words in the same sentence. (For the record, I find it quite irritating for the word *pain* to mosey into the same sentence of a good-feeling word like *joy*.)

Once we search ourselves, intentionally remembering the days of good and bad and the God who reigned over both, we need to press on even further. Our perspective and lens aren't simply looking for Jesus in the good and bad, but also seeing ourselves the way God sees us. We can look back for God's presence in a past situation, but let's move forward in life with the confidence of who we are *in* Christ.

Worthy.

Deeply loved and cherished.

Of course, God doesn't hand us cupcakes while He tells us that life just isn't fair. No, He gives us the perfect balance of truth and grace—like the perfect proportion of wind and tension on a kite string that's needed to pull that kite even higher.

God gives us everything we need. It's not always what we think we need or even what we want, but I'm learning time and time again that His ways are not my ways, and they're actually better than what happens within my rabbit-chasing brain.

Let this go on record. The readings ahead are not scholarly material. They're heart feels and personal experiences. As a nurse who sat in a psych ward for clinical rotations, I have seen firsthand the havoc that is wreaked within people's minds. I have experienced the devastation within myself, as well. That said, this girl 100 percent supports medicinal therapy and other healing outlets that are necessary to treat the chemical imbalances of our minds. It's real. If you need professional help, get it, and do not be ashamed.

As encouragement and betterment exercises for ourselves, we can work through the thoughts and meditations in this book together.

Check It

1: I discovered that the word *remember* is found in the Bible more than two-hundred times. That is more than the words *grace* or *truth*. What is your first thought when you hear this fact? Personally, I was shocked for some reason. Grace and truth seem like some of the "churchiest" words. Something in my abstract mind wonders if the math of our remember-ing leads to balancing of truth and grace. Despite what we think, we can stand firm in the fact that an all-powerful and all-knowing God made no mistakes when it came to word counts in the Bible.

2: Go to www.biblegateway.com and search for the word *remember*. Scroll through all the verses where this powerful word is cited. Take note that this word isn't just used in the context of us remembering God, but also of God remembering His people. That's you and me! We are never forgotten.

Affirmation (Come on, sister! Say it loud! Say it proud!)

God, you are with me here.

God, you were with me there.

God, you are with me everywhere in my life.

Through the happy and the hurt, *you are with me,*
and you love me without end.

I'm claiming and acting on these words in
Psalm 77:11–14 (ESV), "I will remember the deeds
of the Lord; yes, I will remember your wonders of
old. I will ponder all your work, and meditate on
your mighty deeds. Your way, O God, is holy.
What god is great like our God? You are the God
who works wonders . . ."

A Touch More Science

TRAUMA BY DEFINITION IS UNBEARABLE AND INTOLERABLE, we're told in Bessel Van Der Kolk's *The Body Keeps the Score: Brain, Mind, and Body in the Healing of Trauma.*[6] I don't adore math, but I am aware that the addends of many heartbreaks in my life do indeed equal to trauma.

It's not only my rocket scientist math skills that bring me to this awareness but physical symptoms I've experienced over the years: A tight and uneasy feeling in my chest. A racing heart and elevated blood pressure that seems to spike out of nowhere. A delayed response time to things that should make me go into fight or flight mode. *Or* I flat out jump into fight or flight mode when I have no need to.

The replaying of traumatic events sets off landmines in my brain.

At times I toss and turn so much at night that I wake up feeling more exhausted than when I went to bed the night before. (And I feel the need to apologize to my sleeping partner, who lovingly sticks out the restless nights with me to assure me that I'm OK and not alone. I love my hubby.)

Given my family's heart history, over this past decade I've had my heart health checked and triple-checked to make sure that all my symptoms aren't flags of a heart attack or an unknown underlying condition. (Our family physician is a saint of a man that we treasure. He so graciously, patiently, and kingdom-mindedly bears with me in my frantic moments.)

The conclusions of all tests continue to come back within normal range. (Praise!) The feelings that implode me at any hour of the day or night to grab my attention and lead me to say, *Whoa! Slow down, slow down!* That's all anxiety within me.

Have you experienced any symptoms like these while you've walked through a devastating season in life? We could get matching tattoos for it because *you're not alone.*

Not only does your sister girl right here work to reverse these trauma-induced anxiety imprints, but much of the United States' population deals with anxiety, as well. The Anxiety and Depression Association of America (ADAA) tells us that each year, forty million adults (19.1 percent of the population) age eighteen and older are affected by anxiety in the United States. Anxiety disorders are the most common of mental illnesses in our country. Anxiety disorders affect 31.9 percent of adolescents between thirteen and eighteen years old.[7]

Those are staggering numbers, are they not? I'm truly baffled by the reality of anxiety that smothers our nation.

If you're a Bible-believing person, then you may not be entirely shocked by the statistics of earthly disconnect and suffering. From the very beginning of the Bible in Genesis, we learn how the world became broken and sin-filled after the first one took place in the garden of Eden.

However, if Bible-believing is not your thing, then you may be appalled by the numbers and all the negative vibes in our world.

Geek out with me for a minute as we look to better grasp the intensity of this raging anxiety that holds many of us prisoner.

I read a book by someone way smarter than me—Dr. Van Der Kolk—who had done highly detailed research on the human body during healing from trauma. A group of individuals were to recount a traumatic event and it was recorded. Next, they were to describe a scenario where they felt safe and in control.[8]

One participant named Marsha was thirteen years out from losing her five-year-old daughter and seven-month-old fetus in a car accident.

Monitors were hooked up to Marsha in order to track her brain activity. She was read the details of her traumatic event. Following the reading, Marsha's heart rate and blood pressure increased. She was then read her script of a time that she felt safe and in control. Following the reading of her safe and in control scenario, there were no changes to Marsha's heart rate or blood pressure. It seems that our bodies do quite the talking when our mouths are closed, and our brains silently run ninety to nothing within.

The biggest area of brain activity during the reading of Marsha's traumatic experience was in the limbic area, or emotional brain—in particular, an area within it called the amygdala. I know, the word *amygdala* sounds like a four-eyed, twenty-eight-legged critter that you might find under a wood pile. However, it turns out that this portion of our brains is pivotal in our decision-making.

"We depend on the amygdala to warn us of impending danger and to activate the body's stress response," Dr. Van Der Kolk writes. "Marsha's study clearly showed that when traumatized people are presented with images, sounds, or thoughts related to their particular experience, the amygdala reacts with alarm—even, as in Marsha's case, thirteen years after the event."[9]

Monitors picked up on the internal reactions that were taking place inside Marsha's body, even though she was fully aware in the moment that she was in the present and resting quietly in a scanner. You see? Time doesn't change our past, but an intentional perspective in each moment most definitely can.

For those of us who smell the perfume of a loved one from the lady who walked by us in Hobby Lobby, or we see a car wreck as we travel to work, our bodies may be triggered and send us into a racing heart and elevated blood pressure state of being. This is exactly what I've been able to connect the dots on within myself. My amygdala sends my body into a tizzy even when I'm 100 percent aware that I'm joyfully shopping for a new throw rug in Hobby Lobby and not currently in my traumatic time.

The dot-to-dot connecting is exactly what landed me with my doctor, who led me to deciphering what, exactly, I could do to cope with the aftermath of trauma that was impacting my daily life. There's no shame in reaching out for help, my friends. We can't love and care for others if we aren't well ourselves. And if you're like me and place guilt on yourself for stepping away to even get help, or make time for yourself to heal and reset, look your beautiful self in the mirror and say, "Girl, please!" Because that ridiculous guilt is straight from Satan and not yours to claim. It took me way too long to figure out that by taking care of myself, I was also taking care of my people—because they need a healthy me. Dealing with the physical anxiety in my life has greatly helped shape my perspective—of myself and those around me. Dare I say that heartache grows our grace-giving muscle?

Back to the study by scholarly individuals in Dr. Van der Kolk's book.

Marsha's scans revealed a significant decrease in the Broca's area of her brain, which is a speech center that is often affected in stroke patients when oxygen supply to that region of the brain is cut off. Or as Dr. Van der Kolk puts it, "Without a functioning Broca's area, you cannot put your thoughts and feelings into words."[10] When people say, "I have no words" following something surprising or traumatic, they're not lying. If there's no oxygen to that region of the brain then there's also no output.

The science that backs the saying *I have no words* is incredibly wowing to me. On countless occasions, I have sat in front of Austin or other friends and felt like an all-out crazy person. I knew that I needed to release all the pressures building within my heart and mind but I just couldn't add words together to form sentences. And I *always* have something to say—just ask Austin!

In Marsha's study, doctors could make interpretations from several different perspectives that could lead them into deciding on a treatment plan. One option was to try drugs that would subdue her reaction, or possibly even reset her chemical equilibrium. Another was to desensitize her reaction through therapy. Both options were valid.

Just in the way that science can configure different perspectives for the way people handle and deal with trauma and stress following recordings and scans of the brain, we, too, can have awareness of our situation and switch our perspective as we live beyond those stressors and traumatic events. Desensitization helps patients to remember that "that was then and this is now." When we view life from a biblical perspective, we move three steps even further as we acknowledge that God was with us *then*, He is with us in the *now*, and He will be with us *every minute moving forward*!

All right, I'm taking off my lab coat and spectacles. This is the finale of my nosedive into neuroscience. The writeups ahead are sure to stay as lighthearted and laugh-inducing *as possible*, given the facts. Not one of us is alone in our suffering. If something triggers you in the pages ahead, absolutely step away if need be. If you need to go straight to the end of the chapter and read that affirmation piece over and over, then do it. I've done it myself—and I know the unfolding of each chapter in this book. But when we need the space and grace, we must respect the need.

Be kind to yourself.

And remember, we're going to walk through all of it together.

Check It

1: We've learned that our bodies often speak even when our lips don't move. When is a time that your mind was triggered of a past traumatic experience? Now, where do you remember seeing God in that moment? (Example: Maybe it's the simple fact that He kept breath in your lungs during that heart pounding event.)

2: If you, too, feel symptoms of being overwhelmed or anxious in life, what are you doing to help yourself cope and overcome?

Affirmation (Come on, sister! Say it loud! Say it proud!)

God, you are with me here.

God, you were with me there.

God, you are with me everywhere in my life.

Through the happy and the hurt, *you are with me,*
and you love me without end.

I'm claiming and acting on these words in Psalm 77:11–14 (ESV), "I will remember the deeds of the Lord; yes, I will remember your wonders of old. I will ponder all your work, and meditate on your mighty deeds. Your way, O God, is holy. What god is great like our God? You are the God who works wonders . . ."

The Big Check

begin by laying this card down, face up. For you to grasp the validity and grit in the cards I play in the chapters ahead, I need you to see this card first.

I'm an earthly orphan.

Unfortunately, many of us from all walks of life and age ranges possess this card of being orphaned in life by kin or by heart-connected mentors. And if you aren't currently holding it in your hand of life's cards, there will be a day it will be dealt to you. It comes to us all in some shape or form.

If it sounds depressing, empty, and painful, that's because it is. And I know I'm not alone in holding this card in life. Some of us may not have knighted our parents as the most influential and wise people. I did. My momma and daddy were held to the highest and most respected regard by me. But blood-related or not, the people who are older and impart great wisdom on, us typically leave this earth before we do.

I received the first pass of this book's manuscript from my editor in March of 2022. My momentum was strong.

The very next month, I was stirring a pot of portobello pasta sauce over the stove when my phone rang and on the other end of the line my momma said, "Lauren, I have cancer."

If you've never heard that *C* word from a friend or loved one, count it a blessing. If you have, then you know it knocks the breath out of you and feels like you suddenly swallowed a golf ball–sized rock that lodged right in the center of your throat.

"God, this isn't real, is it? We just lost Daddy less than four years ago," I spouted off to the Creator of the world. "Our family needs Momma! Surely this isn't going to end with my being left on earth without parents at thirty-five years old!" Yes, I did.

The forced smiles and "It's OK" commentary I delivered to my children and those around us hung over a current of silent screaming and sugarcoated fury.

I wrote an entire manuscript knowing I stood firmly and wholeheartedly on the encouraging words I'd already sent off for a round-one edit. But after my mother was diagnosed with a very progressed and unknown type of cancer, I lost touch with my own hard-won wisdom. I was now being forced to check my perspective and remember who I knew God to be: a faithful Father of the past . . . and now of the unknown future.

Following Momma's cancer diagnosis, I immediately put all book business to the back burner—and will forever sing praises of my editor and friend who extended heaping doses of grace—so I could be all in as a daughter and caretaker. Just when we seemed to be gaining some traction on life, following Daddy's passing, a rock fall took place right beneath my family's feet.

Life can change in an instant. So can our perspective.

But wait! Wait! Don't close the book and run!

We're not going to wallow in doom and gloom. If you've ever been buried in the sand while enjoying a beautiful beach day, you'll get this. When we playfully get buried in the sand, all that's left showing is our head above our sand-packed bodies. This book—the perspective, the meditations, the affirmations—will feel like the warmth of the sun above coupled with the sound of waves against the shoreline. Relaxing. Soothing. Life-infusing. But there will be moments where the packed sand feels uncomfortable. It itches us in places where the sun doesn't shine, and it can feel suffocating. Yet we will always be able to release these discomforts and continue to laugh and enjoy life with our beach-going buddies.

Come on, let's get to shoveling that wet sand onto our bellies. (Interpretation: Let's start to unpack and repack the moments of our existence—happy ones and hard ones.)

Momma and I talked no less than three times a day. For the previous two years, I saw her at her house twice a day in addition to those phone calls. Following my daddy's passing, Momma purchased a home two doors down from ours. Our children all but ran a dirt line in the neighbor's yard between us as they frequented their

Yaya's house for hugs, invitations to walk around the neighborhood, and to ask for the fun snacks that my husband and I refuse to pay for but that Yaya stockpiled just for them. The girlies often colored pictures for her or would go down to read a book with her. During my girls' homeschooling year, we had Princesses on Parade day on Fridays each week, where they would spend time cooking, crafting, and sewing with grandparents. It was a really nice gig because not only did our preschool-aged daughter and I get to spend some one-on-one time together from the distracted teaching hours on a school day, but Austin and I totally benefited from yummy dinners and crafts that our twins and their grandparents constructed together. Our family was constant and engaged.

As a nurse, I had never even heard of an *unknown* cancer. I accept the fact that doctors can't explain why some people get cancer and others don't, but to not even know a name or where the nasty, mutated cells originated from seemed cruel.

Maybe you're wondering, *Well, how do you treat cancer if you don't know exactly what kind it is?* Excellent question. And the sorry answer is *you can't.* It's like cooking a stranger's favorite meal without knowing their exact preferences and key ingredients. You just start throwing in all kinds of spices, meats, veggies, sauces, and so on and hope the outcome will be a desirable one. That's how treatment went for my momma's unknown cancer. Week after week, she bravely occupied her chemo chair to receive treatments. She was never comfortable. The progressed, unknown cancer was brutal. The oncologists did everything they could, giving her a large umbrella chemotherapy they hoped would attack the no-name cancer in some shape or form. The chemo knocked her down hard. Her quality of life was diminishing. So was the hope of all of us—me, family members, and friends.

If you've never been to a chemotherapy room, here's a peek behind the entryway door. Patients lie in recliners hooked up to potent chemotherapy medications, and they fight for their lives. They might be visiting with a loved one, sleeping, working a word puzzle, or munching on Ritz crackers if it's a good day and they can stomach something of substance. Or patients may be using every ounce of strength they have to not hurl.

When a patient completes their final round of chemo, there is a bell to ring as they exit the treatment area. This doesn't signify that their cancer is completely eradicated, but it does signify completion of a marathon that was bravely endured and is completed for the time being. For some patients it's fifteen doses of ferocious medications designed to kill everything in the path of their cancer-filled body. Other cancer warriors will have to endure even more. Regardless of their chemotherapy infusion counts, the victory walks to the bell are sweet.

One emotional day, Momma and I witnessed the *ding, dong, ding, dong* that echoed through a chilly room of chemo patients. Nurses, fellow cancer patients, and loved ones of the patient all erupted with clapping and *woo-hoos* to join the celebration of a finish line crossed. That afternoon, I witnessed Momma scooch up in her recliner a little taller and saw a spark of hope glisten in her eyes as she saw physical encouragement to keep pressing forward in her pain-filled and exhausting fight. A fire (though momentary) was lit within her because of encouragement from a stranger ringing a bell on the wall.

It was then that God stirred in me and said, *Do you see the hope that comes when we share our journeys with others?* I thought about how the world we live in is just like an infusion room filled with patients. We each have our own individual battles. Some of our battles are known and have good odds; other times we're completely blindsided by our circumstance and our chances of overcoming trial are a complete tossup.

Friends, we must ring our bells of hope when we finish the hard things in life.

Maybe it's the newborn season of motherhood for a neighbor and she simply needs to hear she won't be enslaved to bottle-washing and diapering forever. Whether we're mamas that are years ahead of that parenting season or we're just a few months ahead, our words of empowerment and hope to a sleep-deprived friend should flow like the Mississippi River—constant and freely.

If we've just walked through a season of caring for a loved one with a chronic illness, let's encourage our coworker who drinks her third cup of coffee in the break room because it's all she can do to stay alert and present. We can assure her that every day won't always look and feel like the one she is trudging through as the primary caregiver and breadwinner of her family. Those pressures will let up at some point. There is hope for better days ahead.

Those brief but inspirational moments of ringing our bells of hope can switch someone's perspective on a dime.

My sister, Melissa, and I accompanied Momma to chemo treatments, blood draws, and procedures. We stayed within a six-foot radius of her for all hospital stays—during the day and throughout the night. Melissa and I wrote out everchanging med schedules and packed pill boxes. Our children crafted get-well cards and prayed for their Yaya's tummy to not hurt anymore. Our husbands ran the circus acts at our homes during our absence. And that was *a lot*. It felt like three *long* months—but my perspective now reveals it was terribly short.

Countless friends and family members came alongside us helping with Momma, interceding in prayer, taking loads off our plates at home via meals, providing cleaning help, and playdates for our girls. Our family was doing everything in our earthly power to help Momma beat cancer. Ever since she'd lost Daddy—the very yin to her yang—in 2018, Momma walked through life with an unhealable void in her heart. And despite her yearning to just be with Daddy again, she fought *hard* for three months. Not for herself, but for those she loved.

Momma never got to ring the bell in the chemo room. Her celebration wasn't in a medical facility surrounded by sick people. Instead, it was in the form of complete physical healing in the presence of Jesus and the souls who had already reached heaven. She went running into the arms of Jesus and my Daddy on July 1, less than three months from her cancer diagnosis.

Life is brutal. One minute you're on track to success and happiness, the next minute you can't even form a complete thought following a traumatic event.

Science can explain a lot. As you know, I'm a big fan of anatomy and physiology and fascinated by science-y fun—but I'm here to tell you it has failed me a lot over the last decade of my life. I am thankful that the doctors who had the loudest voices to me and my family were believers in Jesus. When the science failed them and couldn't progress any further, they comforted us and affirmed that God's presence would not fail us despite all the medical world's shortcomings. Their words helped me to check my perspective time and time again. Remembering the good God of the past and believing Him as the same good God of that day was my constant target.

Even on the days when it was all I could do to focus on cutting up strawberries and interacting with my children for thirty minutes without crying or yelling from my undercurrent of pain, God was faithfully present and still holding the world in orbit.

My momma may not have rung her bell down here on earth, but I'm going to chime my hope bell collection louder than opening ceremonies at the Olympics. Sister, I may not always be cheering with dry eyes, but you better believe I'm beside you and rallying you on, nonetheless.

Check It

1: Are you viewing the good and bad times of your life through the lens of a biblical perspective?

2: Think of three people that you see on a weekly basis. Family members, coworkers, friends from your workout class. Keep in mind what they are currently working through in life and if you have some wisdom and past experience in that same arena, ring your hope bell! Words of encouragement can bring life to a suffocating soul.

Affirmation (Come on, sister! Say it loud! Say it proud!)

God, you are with me here.

God, you were with me there.

God, you are with me everywhere in my life.

Through the happy and the hurt, *you are with me,*
and you love me without end.

I'm claiming and acting on these words in
Psalm 77:11–14 (ESV), "I will remember the deeds
of the Lord; yes, I will remember your wonders of
old. I will ponder all your work, and meditate on
your mighty deeds. Your way, O God, is holy.
What god is great like our God? You are the God
who works wonders . . ."

PART 2

Breathable Enhancements

Why?

IS EARS PERK. THE BLIND MAN SITS UP A LITTLE STRAIGHTER as the sound of footsteps and voices grow from far to near. It's more than a couple of men walking together in a group, from what he can gather.

"What did this guy do wrong to have been born blind? Or was it his parents that did something wrong and led to their son being blind?" asked one of the passersby.

"Neither," came the response from the leader of the pack. "This came about so that God's works might be displayed in him."

The leader bent down, spit, and created mud from his warm saliva and the dirt below his feet. He took the mud and smeared it on the eyes of the sightless. He said, "Go and wash your eyes in the pool of Siloam."

The blind man did as he was told. He scooped up the water and washed the sludge from his eyes. And he could see. For the first time he could see the body of water from which he had splashed his face.

The no-longer-blind man returned to the crowd.

Now, he not only felt the temperature and pressing of the sun that shone around him, he could see it. A visible image right before his once blacked-out eyes.

On this day, a man not only saw for the first time the light of day, but the Light of the World.

The leader of the man pack that brought sight to the blind man was Jesus. You can read this paraphrased story in John 9 starting in verse 1. I used the CSB version.

Eeww! Saliva mud to the eyes—that's sicko! Why don't you just go ahead and hand over the eye drops and doxycycline?

I hope you know good and well that my nurse brain is tracking with you on those type of thoughts.

So why did the blind man follow through with such cuckoo-sounding orders?

Why not?

If you had lived your entire life without one of the five senses and someone told you to do X in order to gain that sense, would you hesitate to try what they told you to do?

Coming from a girl who has lost her sense of taste and smell with nasty sinus infections in the past, I'd walk and cluck like a chicken around town hall, eat a lizard dipped in chocolate (actually, I might need more time to process this example before acting on it), or have saliva-mud rubbed on my nose and lips, in order to receive my missing taste and smell. The mud on the eyes doesn't seem so crazy when I list the other scenarios, does it?

But seriously. The most important *why* question here is not *Why the goop to the eyes for healing?* but rather, *Why was the man was born blind?* And the profound and complete response from Jesus was that it was not that this man sinned, or his parents, but *that the works of God might be displayed in him.*

Now that's an astonishing answer. Let's save that bite and chew on that food for thought in a bit.

Aren't we just like the disciples who asked the question of why the man was born without sight? Our daily lives are jam packed with whys.

Why is my phone not working?

Why is this happening to me?

Why won't they respond to my texts or calls?

Why are gas prices so high?

Why am I the one having to read this pamphlet "Understanding Cancer"?

Why do family gatherings feel like I took a nosedive into a pool of molasses—it's so thick and awkward?

Though not likely a naughty word that would land us in the principal's office or with a bad rep, this three-letter word *why* can cause our hearts to spiral down quickly into a drain of disgust and wretchedness. That is, if we aren't filtering our questions through a biblical perspective.

Each day we must check ourselves to see which lens of life we're wearing.

In the early morning before too much chaos has hit the fan, we walk out into the world with our rose-colored glasses ready to pass out love, patience, and goodness. Fast-forward ten minutes and we're doing our darnedest to deep breathe and replay our Bible app's daily verse, rather than sitting on our horn and hollering not-so-sweet-somethings as we sit at a standstill in construction traffic. *Psshh.* We toss our rose-gold, love-filled glasses to the back seat—it's time to get down to business and bust out the tortoiseshell, almond-shaped frames of boldness (and borderline insanity). In a few hours, we'll likely be so over the day that we pitch the business frames to the wayside and don our darkest sunglasses in order to hide the exhaustion and turmoil.

Let's face it—we're all a bunch of fashionistas regarding our daily perspective. And that's OK! We need to keep our look fresh and respond to life with different lenses in front of us—but our self-awareness of when and what to change to is most important. If it's a look that is God-honoring and pure, then roll with it. That's always going to be a good look for you and me!

I plopped onto our beige chaise lounge like a sack of potatoes straight out the back of a farmer's Ford pickup. The day had been long and trying but I could still feel blood pulsating through my veins—a reassuring sign that led me to the realization I was still alive despite my mental beatdown.

Our baby was in bed singing her nightly tunes in refusal of surrender to sleep. Our twins were instructed to brush their teeth and read quietly in their beds before their daddy and I went in to say prayers and "tucker" them in. Dropping my cheek to the cushion, I laughed as I saw a toy giraffe wearing a Fancy Nancy dress, sitting in the La-Z-Boy rocker across the room. What I couldn't figure out was which I found to be more comical—the fancy giraffe or the iguana Beanie Baby dressed in a satin bow tie propped beside it. The stuffed animals shared tea over a Little Tikes plastic charcuterie board of blackberries, corn on the cob, pizza slices, and fruit cocktail, prepared by our six-year-old sous-chefs. Only the freshest and finest plastic foods leave from our girls' gourmet play kitchen.

"Why can't I stay up late?" asked a curly-headed twin from behind the couch.

I could feel my attitude in my eyeballs. I closed my eyes in hopes of hiding the intense rolling motion that was going on as I thought, *I hardly consider nine-thirty an early bedtime for someone under the age of seven.* (Hey, I'm fully aware that our sleeping schedules flop in the summer—and for that lack of consistency, I'm not awaiting any parenting awards.)

I digress.

Before I could open my mouth with a cool-calm-and-collected parenting answer, I remembered that this same sweet child hit me with a round of machine gun–style questions in the car earlier that day.

"Can we have a play date with Logan and Kaley?"

"Why do people die?"

"Ahhh! Why is this seatbelt so tight?"

"Why did she get eight slices of apple and I only had seven?" (Y'all, there's a reason I count out crackers, peanuts, grapes, or chocolate chips when packing food for our twins. The competition runs *deep* in all accounts of their daily matters. I had obviously failed elementary math as I prepared snacks on this day).

When the twin's question clip ran out, our two-year-old took a shot at the mommy target.

"Why is the rain wet on the window?"

"Mommy, why does that man have a sign right there?"

After a quick flashback and review of why-questions from earlier that day, I gave myself a firm pep talk before I attempted another bedtime execution. *Answer the kiddo and you can return to this place of rest soon. Keep it short and sweet.*

So I told her exactly what my daddy always told me and my sister—which drove me nuts, by the way. I peeled open my eyes and straightened my spine as I stood up. Hands to my hips as I arched my back in a stretch.

"Well, sister, you know what the Rolling Stones say: You can't always get what you want, but if you try sometime, you just might find you get what you need. And despite your *wanting* to stay up late, your mind and body *need* rest, so rest you will get. Thank goodness you have a big cozy bed to cocoon yourself into."

Ah. The genetic attitude eyeball appeared on the face of our six-year-old. My husband's Mini-Me's do look a touch like me after all. "But Mommy . . ."

I took six steps forward and gently pulled the ombre-headed, puppy-gown–wearing sister to my stomach and gave her a squeeze hug before we headed down the hall.

Why-questions from the kid crowd are inescapable. Regardless of whether or not you have children living under the roof with you, if you see a child in the grocery store, running through the church lobby, or scootering down the street, you're bound to witness a round of verbalized *why* obstacles. I was 100 percent a *why* child myself—and decades later, I've yet to grow out of it.

What about you?

Austin's boot tapped up and down as he held my hand from the side of the exam table. Paper crinkled and tore below my back as my nervous-self continued to sweat in anticipation of the doctor's arrival.

During the thirteen plus months leading up to this moment, Austin and I had been ambushed with defeat and sorrow.

We had suffered back-to-back miscarriages.

The number of days that I could be found sitting in a bathroom, hunched over cramping and bleeding, crying out *Why?* to God is more than I want to be able to compute. We knew that God had given us the desires in our hearts—and we knew those desires were to raise children and build a family—but God saw fit to grow us deeply in our faith and teach us a few hundred lessons before He allowed those desires to flourish.

In the beginning, Austin and I had no problem *getting* pregnant. Our problem was *staying* pregnant.

Sister, my heart is completely yours if you've found yourself in the past or are currently wading in the waters of this same infertility storm. For those of us who endure these obstacles to parenthood, the why-questions seem to be as numbered as the fish in the sea—they're countless and vary in depth.

Following months of not being able to *stay* pregnant, our problems warped into something completely new. We found ourselves in a new place where we couldn't *get* pregnant.

Austin spent several faithful months standing bedside to me at our own home, with syringes and vials in hand as he administered fertility medications into my what was then a fit and toned torso. The medications were successful in growing my eggs to a size that would be able to sustain a pregnancy once fertilized. However, the meeting of "the tadpole and the egg" just wasn't happening. We were taking meds and playing hanky-panky like clockwork on the calendar, yet each pregnancy test continued to reveal a double negative sign.

I can assure you at this point, I was asking God a lot of why-questions on our journey to parenthood. My perspective was changing by the hour. Hope turned to doubt. Doubt twisted to a moment of unwavering faith in a God who only wants good for His children, followed by a splat of anger and loneliness.

But as I lay heart pounding and sluggish at this particular doctor's appointment, I was wearing my rose-colored lenses on life. It was surprisingly a positive sign on a pregnancy test that had landed us in that exam room. I'm going to give you the whole shebang here. After months of no pregnancy, lots of dollars out, and lots of needle pokes and medications in, Austin and I needed a break—for our hearts, minds, and bank account. Our prayers at that time were for God to give us clarity: for Him to soften our hearts for what it is He had planned for our family, and for some durn peace in the madness. We took a few months off from all medications and doctors. We attended the wedding of a dear friend, followed by a weekend in Memphis, Tennessee, complete with the Beale Street experience and a lot of shimmy shakin' dancing at Justin Timberlake's 20/20 concert. A few weeks later is when our positive pregnancy test was revealed.

Our doctor entered the room at a predictably unpredictable time in perfect medical world fashion. We had done this act a thousand times by now—a monstrous ultrasound probe that doesn't go on your belly was pretty standard in our book. Throughout the first couple of minutes, he made small talk as he twisted and tilted the probe to reveal my uterus innards. This wasn't the doctor we saw on a regular basis, but we were thrilled to have our pregnancy confirmed by whatever knowledgeable physician we could get in with.

"Well, you're definitely pregnant," came the voice from the land down under.

Austin and I looked at each other with crazy excited faces but still holding our breath as we could tell the doctor wasn't finished with his thought.

"There are actually *two* heartbeats here. So you're having twins. Identical twins. Congratulations!"

Oh, buddy that is a moment in time we will *never* forget. My memory is foggy of all the chatter between the pregnancy confirmation and the next portion of the conversation. I imagine Austin and I were trying to wrap our minds around the fact that we had two babies sharing the same womb/room only separated by a thin membrane. (Which was actually a huge blessing. Knowing now how competitive our sisters are, God knew what He was doing by putting up that safety net membrane from the get-go.)

The doctor took off his gloves and began to print the first picture of our rainbow babies. "With identical babies, it's simply the split of one fertilized egg. Science can't explain *why* one egg grows to a particular size and then splits. It just is what it is." (Revisit the shimmy shakin' that went down at Justin Timberlake's concert. That egg just shook all it could until it split in half! I'm kidding. That's not science, y'all.)

It's funny. For being a *why* kid all my life, in this pivotal moment of an indescribable event, my heart was so at peace. And confident.

Austin and I didn't need to know why.

That three-letter word *why* was a firm and undeniable stamp of another three-letter word.

GOD.

Austin and I stepped back from the baby-making world/obsession following our miscarriages and pregnancy hurdles and pressed further into our relationship with the Lord. We learned more about God's will being done and not our own. All the money, time, medications, lost babies, timed sex life, days of yearning and questioning—it all seemed like such unnecessary heartache and an agonizing process, but God revealed to us His complete and flawless timing. And now that we're years out from that experience, our perspective spotlights God's hand on us throughout each turn of events.

And all for His glory. Just like Jesus answered His disciples in John 9, the miracle of our twins, Atalie and Emmie, came about so that God's works could be displayed.

You better believe we shout this witnessed miracle(s) to the rooftops every chance we get.

To God be the glory for the things He has done!

From the healing of a blind man to the raising of a dead man named Lazarus in the book of John, God will receive the glory for the glorified, unimaginable instances in life. I look in wonder (and at times, irritation) into the hazel eyes of three, breathtakingly beautiful daughters each day. Our girlies are my world.

Yes, they take me down with their unending why-questions, but their ponderings remind me that a child's mind is so innocent and wise. Children ask questions from an authentic place of curiosity and marveling. Unfortunately, too often our world tries to place shame on the lives of those who are fascinated, joyful, and free at heart with the world they're in. Next thing you know, we're in middle school and too afraid to ask a question for fear that we'll be laughed at or made fun of. Belittling the inquisitive is no good.

"As a deer longs for flowing streams, so I long for you, God. I thirst for God, the living God. When can I come and appear before God? My tears have been my food day and night, while all day long people say to me, 'Where is your God?' I remember this as I pour out my heart: how I walked with many, leading the festive procession to the house of God, with joyful and thankful shouts. *Why*, my soul, are you so dejected? *Why* are you in such turmoil? Put your hope in God, for I will still praise him, my Savior and my God. I am deeply depressed; therefore I remember you from the land of Jordan and the peaks of Hermon, from Mount Mizar. Deep calls to deep in the roar of your waterfalls; all your breakers and your billows have swept over me. The LORD will send his faithful love by day; his song will be with me in the night—a prayer to the God of my life. I will say to God, my rock, '*Why* have you forgotten me? *Why* must I go about in sorrow because of the enemy's oppression?' My adversaries taunt me, as if crushing my bones, while all day long they say to me, 'Where is your God?' *Why*, my soul, are you so dejected? *Why* are you in such turmoil? Put your hope in God, for I will still praise him, my Savior and my God" (Psalm 42:1–11, CSB, emphases mine).

In the above verses, we can see that faith asks questions. So if we want to live a life worthy of Christ and one that will point all arrows and flashing lights to His namesake, we need to know what we're talking about. We need a more childlike approach. Jesus even tells us to have childlike faith. We need to run from our easily-shamed-and-sheepish chair that we're sitting in and instead, plop our tushes down with the mindset and asking power of our kindergarten-aged selves. We should ask the questions without fear of the mockery that could follow. Let's not take things at face value—let's check and challenge facts against the morals we were taught and the scriptures in God's word.

Let's address the big question: But *why* do bad things happen?

Y'all, I don't have a pretty answer for that. Though true, the answer I have can feel very hurtful or even lead to resentment if we're caught in a moment of wearing the wrong lens in life. When our perspective is fuzzy, the truth seems to pierce deeper.

I've begged God for a lot in my life. Healing, understanding, help in the unthinkable—and though His answer was not always what I wish it would have been, I can say that God is good. Just like Jesus told His disciples about the blind man, our circumstances aren't always caused by our own action or lack thereof. Again, sometimes the only answer is the one that Jesus gave in John 9: "This came about so that God's works might be displayed in Him" (v. 3, CSB). God is loving. He is trustworthy. He is gracious. He will work all things for the good of those who trust in Him—and it's all in His timing and for His glory.

Is it easy to press forward in life with all our why-questions that may not be clearly answered while we live on earth? Heck, no. But nothing worth having in life comes easy.

Let's keep asking the "why" questions like Jesus's disciples and the children of our world. From our questioning, our hearts grow, our wisdom deepens, our Biblical wonderings become more clear, and God's Kingdom can grow!

Check It

1: Is there a particular question you are consistently bringing to God in this season of your life? (Maybe you feel like He's on vacation and not listening, but sister, He's listening and holding you as you continue to present your question. In God's perfect time, He will reveal an answer.)

2: If you're like me, sometimes it feels impossible that God can bring good from our hurts and questioning (even though we can recount from times passed where He brought good out of our not so good feels and experiences). Revisit John chapter 9 and continue to tell yourself that God will receive the glory from the hard and unknown. Is there a friend you could pray with during your waiting season?

Affirmation (Come on, sister! Say it loud! Say it proud!)

God, you are with me here.

God, you were with me there.

God, you are with me everywhere in my life.

Through the happy and the hurt, *you are with me*,
and you love me without end.

I'm claiming and acting on these words in
Psalm 77:11–14 (ESV), "I will remember the deeds
of the Lord; yes, I will remember your wonders of
old. I will ponder all your work, and meditate on
your mighty deeds. Your way, O God, is holy.
What god is great like our God? You are the God
who works wonders . . ."

Tinkerbell and Eeyore

"*HONEY, THIS IS SUCH A HARD CHAPTER FOR ME TO* write." These were the words I vulnerably released to my husband, Austin, as he asked how my writing for this book was coming along.

"Why's that?"

"Because I'm writing about you and I'm afraid my words won't do you justice—that they won't be good enough."

"They won't," he said with a straight face.

This coming from the man who is so good to give me doses of truth when he tells me that he can't hear the words that I'm saying over my attitude. And now he's giving me lip?

I pursed my lips and put my hands on my hips. I had all but cursed him in my mind before his mischievous smile appeared.

"Hey, seriously. You're doing an incredible job. The only one telling you that you're not going to do good enough is you. Be kind to yourself. You got this, babe."

My Austin is breathtakingly witty. Highly uplifting. Often borderline inappropriate. Eye candy, no doubt. And insanely compassionate.

I love this person of mine.

We all have "our people" in life who keep us on our toes and ultimately carry us on the days when we mentally, emotionally, or physically can't push forward.

Austin is that person for me.

For you, it may be a friend from high school who has never lost touch, despite the hundreds of miles of farmland that separate you.

Your person may be a family member who has been more like a friend to you all your life.

We all have our people and we all need to have those people on speed dial, because when our life hits a sinkhole—and I mean like losing a loved one, bankruptcy, loneliness, anxiety, troubles at work, any number of things—we need our peoples' voices of reason and encouragement easily accessible. We need their voices of assurance and devotedness to jump in and save us.

Let me shed some light on Austin so you'll understand who he is and how he came about being my person.

Years ago, my 1999 Nissan Maxima and I pulled into my college town after being on Thanksgiving break. Momma and Daddy had instructed me to deliver something to Austin that they had carefully packed in the trunk.

Austin and I had only been on one official date up until this point. Before that, we had simply been friends for two years—now we were friends who were starting to do a lot more life and confiding in one another.

I pulled into Austin's driveway to find him waiting there with a big ol' bear hug. Ten days away from each other is like a lifetime when you're young and in love, right?

I told Austin that Momma and Daddy had a gift for him in the trunk of my car. I'm not sure why he didn't go for the paisley Vera Bradley tote. Rather, he grabbed the black gun case that lay on top of it.

My parents had sent Austin a new 30-06 bolt-action rifle and scope. A look of overwhelming gratitude and bewilderment appeared across Austin's face. As he tells it, after only going on one official date with me, he had several thoughts spinning in his mind:

"A. Lauren's dad saw me kiss his daughter. This gun as a 'present' is a silent threat.

"B. Lauren's dad is in the CIA and I'm %$#@ed.

"C. By nature, Lauren's parents are conduits for relationships. They know how to connect people because they know everything about everyone around them. Because of the intensity of this gift, and my lack of experience receiving gifts in such a way, I assume I owe them for this. Problem: I am broke, so how could I ever pay them back? I'm %$#@ed.

"D. This gun must've been used in a crime, and this is how they're going to get rid of me—planting the gun in my possession then calling the cops once my fingerprints are on it.

"E. Run! Or . . .

"F. Lauren's parents are genuine givers who desire the best for their daughter, and despite the reflection of who I see myself as in the mirror, they see me as someone with promising potential. They have faith in me to be the right man."

After his phone call of gratitude to my parents, Austin realized that option *F* was the answer. My parents had been told about Austin hunting with borrowed rifles, and they weren't going to let that be the case any longer. Momma and Daddy have had irrational giving hearts all of their lives. They wanted Austin to have ownership of his hunting equipment. To feel loved and proud from a physical gift that was *his own*. This gift exchange was a gamechanger in our relationship. It revealed the hearts and sincerity of my parents to Austin. And it spoke volumes to me about the trust and love that my parents had for him.

I can't say that I'm against arranged marriages. I'm happily fourteen years into an arranged wedlock myself. *Wink wink!*

Turns out, my parents realized that Austin would be my forever person before I did. I found myself in the familiar boat of *Momma and Daddy know what's best* that I have ventured in all of my life—and it's true. They picked the perfect guy for me.

Today, I don't have enough words of gratitude and consensus for Momma and Daddy, in their choosing of my Prince Charming. But the hot and bothered lovey-dovey sensations that I get when I'm with Austin is not on a switch my parents could turn on.

Our unshakable friendship and love story was ultimately God's plan playing out.

My honey once referred to our coupling status as Eeyore and Tinkerbell.

He's my Eeyore and I'm his Tink.

Disney references earn him major bonus points in our book of love. To my surprise, the Tinkerbell traits of sassy, feisty, and stubborn parallel precisely with my personality.

Though Austin doesn't currently have floppy ears like Eeyore, I'm holding out that one day when we're in our seventies, his ear elasticity will give way.

I assume he calls himself Eeyore because his facial expressions aren't (and probably never will be) a plastered smile and the expression of a cheerleader catching flies with his/her mouth on ESPN's latest cheer competition. I don't think he gives himself enough credit in the fun-loving and free-spirited department though. Y'all, he's the baby of four boys—and if you understand the birth order then you understand that bottled up inside his Mr.-Tough-Guy-business-all-the-time self is an outgoing, charming, and easygoing man who loves to be set loose.

Even more interesting is that we switch roles of who mindfully mopes around like Eeyore and who leaves a trail of illuminating pixie dust. I certainly have my days of hammering that donkey tail onto my rear, and Austin is quite debonair with sparkly wings. Our daily ensemble of donkey or fairy depends on our individual perspectives in the day.

What I love about God's design of human relationships is how they balance each other in perfect ratios. Whether you're thinking about you and your spouse, or you and your best friend, you're probably able to see the similarities and differences within your friendship.

It's the fun surprises of combinations that makes life sweet. Like a Reese's Cup smothered between a roasted marshmallow and crisp graham cracker, instead of making a s'more using the standard Hershey's chocolate bar. Seriously, go try that combo and see if it doesn't leave you salivating for more.

I can't help but think that if we made a habit of cleaning our life lens and refocusing our perspective on the story God has written for each of us, we might find the odd and confusing moments to be some of the most surprising and treasured. That's the view that has been coming into focus for me within the last few years.

Austin is so good to remind me to check my point of view.

As I look back through my grief journey after losing my precious daddy, I have unwanted flashbacks of unwarranted snappiness from me to my family. All overflow from my anxiety and grief. It makes my stomach churn to know those reactions are part of my story, but I can't camp out there.

What I do need to acknowledge and stay focused on are instances in which my family and friends extended an insane amount of grace and composure to me, despite my roller coaster of feelings.

For instance, one early morning around three a.m. I found the entire house was dark, quiet, and asleep. All except for me and baby Julianna.

I had just fed her sweet self and was attempting to get her to go back to sleep. Salty hot tears were pouring down my cheeks as I bounced and swayed her back and forth in our master bathroom. The constant motion and overhead noise of the bathroom fan was the only combination that kept her asleep. If I even attempted to set her down in the bassinet, she caused quite the ruckus.

It was in those wee hours of the mornings when everyone else in the house was sound asleep and the rooms were dark, that Satan weaseled his way into my every thought channel. On this morning, I felt like I was suffocating from loneliness—down in the bottom of a deep, dark well, so quiet I could hear the eyelids blinking on the toad next to me.

I guess I wasn't doing as good a job as I thought keeping my crying silent because Austin appeared through the French doors of the bathroom. "Honey, what's wrong?" he asked through squinted eyes.

My mind was racing a million miles an hour in seven different directions. We were freshly home from the hospital with a baby who had endured an open-heart surgery and my daddy had passed a short four months before. I hadn't even had time to fully process the reality of these events in my life.

It was hard to even corral my thoughts on how to answer Austin's question, so I made the brilliant decision to just let my mouth open before I actually thought.

Through tears and pig-snort crying I responded, "I just feel so lonely! Leave me alone!"

Did you catch that? "I just feel so *lonely*! Leave me *alone*!"

That's how much of a dark and irrational hold Satan had on me. I was weighed down by loneliness, yet I asked to be left alone. That's just dumb. (But don't tell our daughters I said that! It's a Do Not Use bad word that is written in the bylaws of our family.)

Why should Austin have to take on the exhaustion and despair I was wrestling with? I wanted him to leave me to drown in my solitude at three a.m.

But he wouldn't. Throughout all our years of loss and struggle, Austin and I have always grieved in our own *individual* ways but always endured the grieving road *together*.

Austin's love and understanding of my broken heart at three a.m. kept him from rolling over and returning to his slumber. Instead, he sat straight up in the bed and began to speak God's words of acceptance, strength, and mercy over me even though I was far from acceptant of them but in dire need of their healing.

He always makes me feel so safe. So seen. So desired. Even when Satan tells me I'm an undesirable, unseen individual in grave danger.

Find your people who will detour from their own comfort and pleasure to help you pick up the shattered pieces of your heart. Don't push them away when you're down and depressed. That's exactly what our enemy wants us to do—but that's when he can drain the very life and sanity from us. Believe me. I've been there.

If you're like me and have that "who/what/where/ when/why, I just have to know some facts before I believe it" mentality, then I have a treasure piece of scripture for you.

Isaiah 43:1–2 tells us, "Fear not, for I have redeemed you; I have called you by name, you are mine. When you pass through the waters, I will be with you; and through the rivers, they shall not overwhelm you; when you walk through fire you shall not be burned, and the flame shall not consume you" (ESV).

That's truth for you and for me. *God is always with us.* Hardships and struggle will ebb and flow through our life stories, but we will not be consumed by them because God's love and grace is the consuming factor. Lock arms with the folks who know and believe that truth and have no holdbacks of speaking it over you.

A few lines below that scripture in Isaiah 43, verse 4 says, "I love you."

God's words over us. Right there in black and white in the greatest history book of the world that has yet to be disproven. The Bible is repeatedly affirmed by artifacts and words.

If you don't often hear the words, "I love you" from someone, first hear me say that I love you. As your sister in Christ, I love you and want you to know that you're not alone. You don't have to cry at three in the morning while Satan has a heyday in your mind making you feel isolated and unwanted. Those are lies and trash talk.

Secondly, when you need to hear those loving words, pull out your Bible and turn to Isaiah 43:4 (ESV). Highlight it. Read the verse aloud over yourself: "Because you are precious in my eyes, and honored, and I love you."

You, my friend, are very loved.

If your life isn't feeling so sparkly and attractive but rather dull and shattered, you're not alone. We all have our share of Eeyore moments full of moping and moaning, "Nobody likes me" and "Don't worry about me. Go and enjoy yourself. I'll stay here and be miserable" times.

On the flip side, we'll also have our sassy and sweet Tinkerbell occasions, where we fly high in life's happy current, bedazzling everyone around us with splashes of energy, and crossed armed attitudes as to say, "I don't have an attitude problem, I just have a personality you can't handle."

Perspective through it all is of highest priority. The people we allow to influence our perspective is paramount.

Some of us already have an Austin-like confidant.

Some of us are still waiting for that perfect someone to intersect with our lives. Regardless of our current "people" status, we have the ever-present and never-ending love and compassion of our God.

We always have and always will.

Remember what God said to you in Isaiah 43:4: "I love *you*."

Check It

1: Who are your people in life right now? Take a minute to write them a note or send a text of thanks!

2: Do you fully believe in the words of Isaiah 43? How could you incorporate these words of love into your every day as a reminder? Sticky notes on mirrors and calendars? The possibilities are endless.

Affirmation (Come on, sister! Say it loud! Say it proud!)

God, you are with me here.

God, you were with me there.

God, you are with me everywhere in my life.

Through the happy and the hurt, *you are with me,*
and you love me without end.

I'm claiming and acting on these words in
Psalm 77:11–14 (ESV), "I will remember the deeds
of the Lord; yes, I will remember your wonders of
old. I will ponder all your work, and meditate on
your mighty deeds. Your way, O God, is holy.
What god is great like our God? You are the God
who works wonders . . ."

For You I Will

PLEASE TELL ME THAT I HAVE SOME FELLOW MILLENNIALS who read the chapter title and continued on with Monica's late '90s lyrics. I have some strong flashbacks of that song playing at our middle school dances. You know, the ones where boys held up one side of the building hoping that the speaker system would bust, and the dance would end. All the while the girls stood across the dance floor, gathered in circles to giggle and hope for a slow dance invitation . . . once we got back from rinsing out our retainers after that legendary crockpot cheese dip and Fritos corn chips, of course.

Pop R&B artist Monica may or may not have grasped it in the '90s, but the compounding of the words *for you I will* can be life-changing.

For me, it has flip-flopped my everyday thought process and perspective.

From sitting around a dining table with family members who won't even make eye contact with me, to the zombie walks across the house at two in the morning to console a teething child, it's my new perspective on the for-you-I-will motive that helps to keep me in a forward motion. All my life, I've had that standard in my daily living, though for way too long my for-you-I-will was to make other people happy. I was a queen of people-pleasing.

To be altruistic is to have or show an unselfish concern for the welfare of others.[11] If you ever hear of this term regarding the animal world, it goes as far as saying that the behavior of the animal may actually cause the individual animal harm but will benefit the species around them. That's some selflessness—to risk harming yourself for the love of others.

An altruistic police officer risks their life to save others when they're caught in the cross fire of a hostage situation. An altruistic sibling gives her last ticket for the merry-go-round to her sister so she can experience the joy from the ride one last time.

It's not a bad thing to want to please and do good for others, but it's critical to know the motives driving us in our do-good rhythms.

I can't tell you that mine were always rational.

When I was growing up, my sweet daddy was so outnumbered in our house. My momma, baby sister, and I kept the house exciting with all of our estrogen-filled shenanigans and feelings. Even our animals were females. The X-chromosome attitudes flowing through the air in our home was so thick, it was hard to breathe at times—or maybe that's because we talked all the time and we couldn't catch a breath—that's beside the point.

Because my daddy didn't have any sons, I told myself that I *really* needed to embrace hobbies alongside him. Even if they seemed like a father-son type activity, I needed to fill that role and be the son that Daddy never had. Turns out, in all my girly-ness, I wholeheartedly loved Daddy's hobbies!

He had zero desire to sit in a deer stand in frigid temperatures while waiting to see if the rustling of leaves behind him was Bambi or Yogi Bear coming to look for a picnic basket. He did, however, love to target shoot.

All my life, you could often find our family on our land, setting up waterfilled two-liter Coke bottles or old milk jugs along a dirt mound. Gunshots could be heard a mile away.

It was thrilling. My momma, sister, and I were pistol-packin' mommas. We would don our ear protector headphones and do some damage to those water jugs. The end result somewhat resembled the fountains at the Bellagio in Vegas—only gone redneck LA style. (That's lower Arkansas for the uninitiated.)

It was during those gatherings at the back of a truck tailgate with a pistol in my hand that I had ample opportunity for laid-back conversation. I learned a great deal about who I was, who my family was, and who my parents believed I was and could become. I deeply treasure the target memories of me and my family. They are some of my sweetest core memories.

We all have those special memories that will forever fill us with wisdom and heart smiles. Each of us has someone or something that we will say "For you I will" to. Firing off six rounds from a Colt .38 special revolver was one of mine.

When pregnant with our twins, I started eating wiggle-jiggle scrambled eggs that I had gagged over and refused to eat for the prior twenty-eight years of my life. I just couldn't get past the texture. But once I learned the developmental benefits that our babies would receive from the egg's choline content, I pushed through the initial retching and began to eat eggs regularly.

It's astonishing. The things we'll do for those we love and want the best for.

Take a minute and think of the church activities, community volunteering, or work committees that you sign up for. Not necessarily because your heart beats daily for the purpose or drive behind those organizations, but because you love someone so deeply who is connected to that cause and you'd do anything for *them*. They are your for-you-I-will.

I'm not saying we should always jot down our John or Jane Hancock on the sign-up sheets. We each need to recognize and set appropriate commitment boundaries. However, I will say that if through those times of togetherness and contributions, you are allowed the space and opportunity to love on and encourage someone else, *do it*. If you find yourself being refueled and uplifted during the volunteer coaching gig or soccer mom snack role, *do it!*

God knew that my character and perspective would grow by leaps and bounds through my for-you-I-will rendezvous, such as target shooting.

I haven't a doubt in my mind that God is using your for-you-I-will cards as avenues to strengthen and grow your heart, soul, and mind as well.

He wants good for you, my friend. He wants you to experience the goodness, joy, and thrill that He experiences when He thinks of *you*, His precious child. You are God's for-you-I-will. (We'll unpack more of that gift later in this chapter.)

I believe that we all have a little void inside our chests—deep inside our very being.

Dagnabbit, the vacancy inside just irritates us, until we figure out what it is that's missing. It's like that single, empty picture frame dangling next to ten complete photo frames. It's an eyesore every time we see it—yet we don't want to throw any old snapshot behind the glass.

A few years back, Austin and I found ourselves in a vacant-feeling, unsettled kind of way with our drive for life. We wondered if what we did every single day had deep purpose.

Austin was building stunning homes for families. I was at our home trying to keep our four walls from needing repair as the twins and I wallowed through glitter, veggie straw crumbs, and toys each day. Our daily goal was to not cause more work for Daddy once he came home.

So we took a class on the world Christian movement at a local church. As God was leading our steps, we felt confident that the class was destined to change our lives in some shape or form.

And it happened. Our hearts were remolded and the trajectory of our faith journeys sky-rocketed in that class. Our minds were blown by the vastness of God's love. Austin and I discovered that the agitating, itchy void within our hearts was made *whole*. For so long we had been focused on our everyday tasks and responsibilities. We were too consumed with how we could best please the people we were doing life with. Our life perspective was skewed.

Maybe you can relate.

Halfway through a semester of sitting under fluorescent bulb lights, surrounded by brothers and sisters in Christ who were yearning for more intimacy and depth with our Creator, the blinders that jaded my daily perspective were ripped away: I had not been playing my for-you-I-will card correctly for too long.

Through my studying of God's word, our world's history, and the spoken testimonies of others, a neon sign lit up in in my brain—*God* should be your number one for-you-I-will. In everything. Monday through Friday. Twenty-four seven. On all holidays and weekends. With God as my for-you-I-will, He will trump and be the main pool of love that all of my other for-you-I-wills flow from in life.

Colossians 3:23 is somewhat of a for-you-I-will definition. It says, "Whatever you do, work heartily, as for the Lord and not for men" (ESV). Situations don't sound so people-pleasing and cumbersome when the core drive within us is to do all good and pleasing works in life for God's glory. Yet humans might belittle our pure efforts and motives, even when we pour every ounce of energy and love into them. And that hurts. Kent M. Keith is a speaker and author who is highly educated and deeply driven to help people find a purposeful life in this crazy world that we live in. As a sophomore in college, Dr. Keith wrote a booklet for high school leaders in hopes of motivating them and shedding light on different methods for working together. This book contained words known as The Paradoxical Commandments (or you may have heard the title referred to as *Anyway*). In a nutshell, these commandments serve as encouragement on how to find meaning in adversity and to continue moving forward in doing good. I love Dr. Keith's words. They're so profound, even Mother Teresa put a copy of the commandments on a wall at her children's home in Calcutta, which speaks volumes of the words found in Dr. Keith's writing. "People are illogical, unreasonable, and self-centered. Love them anyway. If you do good, people will accuse you of selfish ulterior motives. Do good anyway." These are just a couple of Dr. Keith's wise nuggets. If you go online, you can read the full write up.[12]

We are each a one-of-a-kind design. We each have been dealt a variety of life's playing cards depending on our circumstances. Therefore, we all play our cards differently according to our different perspectives.

For some of us, enacting our for-you-I-will card may look like signing up to serve food at the local homeless shelter, because to serve and provide for others is what God calls us to do. The smell of dirt and heart-wrenching sights of incredible need aren't what we go running toward to find fun, but we will step into that space if it's a way to love God and love His people well.

Jesus didn't avoid those who looked different than Him and His disciples. God in the flesh ministered to the diseased, broken, and sinful. He didn't live His three decades on earth to wine and dine with the upper class. God in the flesh didn't play His life cards of working miracles, asking hard questions, and standing in the ruts of life with others to people-please. Jesus did it all to glorify His Father.

We can all use the same method as we hold our life cards. Let's play all in and maximize our time on earth to glorify God.

We choose to continue sitting across the family table and feel the thickness of misunderstanding or anger of one or two people who sit amongst the love and laughter of many others—because for God, we will.

When it's ten at night and all we want to do is binge watch Netflix after a long day of working and being a human, our friend calls to vent as she is going through a nasty divorce and needs to talk. We turn off the tube and put on our best listening ears. Because for God, we will.

It's not about people-pleasing or checking a box on how a "churchy person" should act. It's about exemplifying the fact that we are made in the image of a God who loves, forgives, and cares without bounds. So we will too.

Without expecting anything in return, Jesus extended love, grace, and forgiveness to friends and enemies, as continually as day turns to night.

Who does that?

Each of us are born into this world as helpless babies with instant demands and selfishness. As babies, we learn to expect immediate attention and compensation. When we're cold, we cry. When we're hungry, we cry. When we need to be changed, we cry. When we're tired of being alone (most often between the hours of one a.m. and four a.m.—can I get an amen?), we cry. No one teaches us this response, it's part of our human nature. However, as we grow and mature, we begin to realize the sacrifices made by those who raised us as they met our every need that we couldn't fulfill ourselves.

The same is true in our card game of life and in our target-shooting endeavors. Ultimately, we all have the same end goal or target, but it takes many years of sitting around the table with other players to learn when and how to correctly play our cards. We have to study, experience, and choose firsthand to view life from a perspective of love.

Me? I found the perfect for-you-I-will card hand to be played in my Perspectives on the World Christian Movement class. As I was sitting in a cramped room for eleven consecutive Monday evenings, the Lord so clearly revealed to me that my motives were too much about myself and those around me—and not enough at all about Him.

I had made myself and others more of a priority than my own Creator. I was altruistic towards those around me—but my for-you-I-will was all wacky.

"God, for you I will!"

That feeling of peace and tranquility that you experience as you face west and watch the sun set is an ambience from a God who says, "For *you* I will," as He paints the ombré beauty of pink and orange.

There are a bajillion examples of God's crazy deep love for you. I hope that every time you see a cross symbol on the back of someone's car or tattooed on the ankle of your pizza waitress, you instantly think of and savor the love that Jesus has *for you*. The cross is the ultimate picture of what a for-you-I-will motive or response should be.

Our for-you-I-will should transpire from the longing to bring light into the darkness. Our motives should connect and bring others to life through uplifting and grace-filled actions *and* boundaries.

That reckless, unending, and immeasurable love is exactly what Jesus came to show us on earth. The Son of God healed the blind and the lame. Not because He got a hefty paycheck afterward or had a building named in His honor. He did it from an unfathomable love.

When people asked questions, Jesus didn't belittle and punk them for the sake of His own pride and wit. He leaned in closer to them to listen and offer insight to help. (I know my loose-lipped self can take some notes on that practice of less talking and more listening.)

The only flawless human to walk this earth was mistreated, spit on, mocked, betrayed, and hung on a cross to die. Yet even through the blood, sweat, and beatings, Jesus wanted to do it, and He carried it out to completion so that you and I could have eternal life if we believe in Him.

His target has always been on our restoration. You and I will forever be Jesus's for-you-I-will!

The question is, will He be ours?

Check It

1: Who is your for-you-I-will? If God is one of them, do you have Him correctly placed at the top of your list above all others? I don't always keep mine in an orderly fashion. But I try to remind myself that I'm a human and moving forward in grace-fueled acceleration is what I need to do as I daily reevaluate and rearrange priorities. (Keep your heart's grace tank full so you can offer it to others *and* yourself.)

2: What is one act of kindness or love that you can give out today? Big or little—you get to choose. Then go *do it!*

Affirmation (Come on, sister! Say it loud! Say it proud!)

God, you are with me here.

God, you were with me there.

God, you are with me everywhere in my life.

Through the happy and the hurt, *you are with me*,
and you love me without end.

I'm claiming and acting on these words in
Psalm 77:11–14 (ESV), "I will remember the deeds
of the Lord; yes, I will remember your wonders of
old. I will ponder all your work, and meditate on
your mighty deeds. Your way, O God, is holy.
What god is great like our God? You are the God
who works wonders . . ."

Synchronized Swimming

YOU PULL INTO THE FAST-FOOD DRIVE-THRU WITH HOPES that the ninety-nine–cent chicken pack will calm the tailspin of hangry kiddos in the back seat. While looking out your front windshield you find it fascinating to see the blowing and splattering of humongous rain drops, all while a meteorological phenomenon casts colors across the sky to form a rainbow.

A kaleidoscope of beauty and a surge of rainfall coexist.

Your hair blows in the humid Arkansas breeze as you relax in your hammock, enjoying an evening of stargazing over the rolling, pine-covered Ouachita Mountains. All at once, the world is calm and peaceful. You take a swig of that perfectly sweetened iced tea while simultaneously smashing the big momma mosquito that was feasting on your ankle.

Serenity and inflamed epidermis coexist.

Sweat zigzags between your shoulder blades as you hold that plank for the final thirty seconds of your heated barre class. Your arms and torso are quivering, but you know that it means muscle is being broken down and strengthened so you're good with the bowl-full-of-jelly arm jiggle.

Trembling limbs of burning muscle and pride in your step toward a healthier you coexist.

Joy and pain coexist.

That word combo of joy and pain coexisting has proved to be the epiphany I inked at the top of my list of phrases that have changed me.

Friends, without any bows or "pretties" attached, I just have to say I hate seeing those two words together. A group of feisty nerves start to fire off within me when I see that negative and nasty word *pain* intruding on the bliss and goody feels of the word *joy*.

But for now, that intruding concept of pain must co-exist with joy.

Here on this planet, you can't separate the two, but through the flowing of life, I'm finding my perspective to reveal a less harsh view of the duo.

Imagine yourself as a participant in the Olympic sport of artistic swimming, formerly known as synchronized swimming.

First, you must properly suit up!

Goggles? Check.

Double hair cap to tame and protect your waves of ginger dyed hair and hold down the flappy goggle straps? Check.

Nose clip? That's your call, my friend. I haven't heard of the fashion police being summoned at the latest Olympic games, but I did hop on over to the Google to check out some trends for you. I'm pleased to report that the twenty-first century does offer quite the line of revamped, almost-invisible-looking silicone clips for your snout. Check it!

Now, time to jump in the water.

You and seven other individuals have worked tirelessly to perfect twists and turns both above and below the water's surface. Your toes point to form a lovely C shape. The poise of your side fishtail placement is matched by those to your right and to your left. But as you come up to refill your lungs with air and join hands for a quick star float before entering a barracuda position, you begin to feel a piercing burn within your calves. Perhaps that unsettling, pulling sensation stems from a toe cramp that will vanish soon. You know you're in shape and capable of executing every stretch of your routine, but the physical tax is really starting to register.

You're experiencing several emotions at once while in the thick of an important performance seen all over the world. Yet all the judges and international viewing audiences see is an art form unfolding before their eyes. Synchronized finesse and wonder radiating from a group of eight individuals is the reality the world sees.

Behind the waterproof makeup and sparkle swimsuits are humans. If one rabbit-chasing thought took away their focus, the glimmer would fade and the routine would no longer be in sync. Beauty and trials are in the same frame.

Our lives are much like synchronized swimming.

We don't always wear the gear for it, but our double whammy feels are a reality. We experience erratic currents of sensations and equations, all at once. Grief, pain, joy, excitement, denial, exhaustion, accomplishment, weariness, anxiety, and anger.

The world's view of our life seems timely and in tune. Yet behind our polished skin and seemingly flawless performance in our day to day, we are simultaneously aching and well-pleased. Sometimes we must hold different things in the same hand.

Joy and pain coexist.

My awareness of joy and pain coexisting came out of the most oppressive years of my life.

Our bunco group had pregnancy announcements left and right, yet even after drinking the same water at our game night, my positive pregnancy tests evolved to gloom. Bitterness and defeat permeated my soul.

When Austin and I had two back-to-back miscarriages, our hearts were crushed. My perspective at the time was so out of focus. I looked around me and saw baby announcements on every third Facebook newsfeed. Women with pregnant bellies always seemed to be who waddled in front of me at the grocery store.

But God.

As I've mentioned, God had planned an extremely specific and trying journey for Austin and me to reach parent status and gain a new perspective. He knew that parenthood was the desire of our hearts, but He also knew that we needed to "visit the eye doctor" and have our lenses checked.

Austin and I were brought to our knees in pain. The recurrence of miscarriages was beyond our human comprehension. I had exploratory surgery to provide guidance on what kind of offbeat jig my body was jamming to. We spent months poking and prodding with fertility medications to help us even get pregnant following our miscarriage rounds. Heartfelt pain and physical jabs.

It was on that perfect November day in 2013 that God transitioned our lenses and revealed to us our positive pregnancy test and the ultrasound that showed two flickering heartbeats of love.

And so, a marvelous adventure with our twins, Atalie and Emmie, ensued.

Adjacent to our giddiness in life with twins, Austin and I grieved the lives of our two babies in heaven. We were in a thick of holding joy and pain. On our heavenly babies' due dates and holidays, we wondered what they would look like and what extra sounds would fill our home. But we also experienced immense joy in the pregnancy of our twin daughters. Not only did God gift us with the titles of mommy and daddy that we both longed to wear, but He also brought to life Ephesians 3:20, a verse I had taped to our bathroom mirror throughout our fertility trials: "Now to him who is able to do above and beyond all that we ask or think according to the power that works in us" (CSB).

God had done immeasurably more than we could have ever asked or imagined! You want to talk about blowing the mind of a Southern girl who lived in a saturated culture of church buildings and "bless your hearts," here's where the mic drop occurred.

Joy and pain coexist.

Just like the Olympic artistic swimmers who appear to have it all together and be without a single hiccup, our synchronized routine of suffering was well rehearsed. Outsiders probably didn't see too many offbeats from our daily tasks, but my mind was all kinds of bumfuzzled on the inside.

During this time of joy and pain coexisting I began to coat myself with self-inflicted guilt. A guilt for feeling happy. Though I wanted to truly celebrate the miracle of our identical twins, I was still dealing with indescribable hurt and trauma from the loss of our previous pregnancies.

I wasn't sure how to act, feel, or think.

Anyone else with me on this confusing feeling of having to hold joy and pain in the same hand?

I even asked God why He would allow me such depths of extreme emotions and realities. I wanted to shout to the world about our miraculous, identical twins. And though I did, a little voice continually weaseled its way into my mind and said, *But remember you lost two babies before these babies were created. Don't think that these rainbow babies in your life are such a big deal, because the God you're shouting praises to is the same God that allowed you to be left with empty arms following your first two pregnancies.*

Hindsight is 20/20, right?

When Satan said "But remember," it should have been my cue to stand quicker and more firm on the words of Psalm 77 that assured me of God's presence even in the hurt. I have since learned so much about switching my lens in the face of all Satan's punk statements. He speaks defeat, lies, weariness, and guilt into our thought processes, and he loves every hateful minute of it.

Yes, God didn't bring me and Austin to parenthood in the way that I saw as Facebook-post presentable, but that same God healed my mother's breast cancer in my first year of marriage and put Austin's mom in remission from leukemia.

He's the God who has allowed me to keep breathing despite life's circumstances that have put my entire body in shock and left me hanging by a thread on the arch of faith.

He's sovereign and He has covered me with a peace that is truly indescribable. He has saved my spirit, time, and time, again. He's the God who has bound my wounds and given me scars that serve as reminders of new growth and life within me, from an incident that left me injured and crushed.

We all have battles of joy and pain. Each warfront is unique, but at the core, joy and pain have equal, coordinated roles throughout. Our perspective plays a major role in the process.

First and foremost, do we stop and take the time to look for the joyful moments that are sprinkled among our hurts?

It can be downright hard to do when the pain we're feeling is so intense. Sometimes moments of delight can only be seen from a microscope's view. Other times, a never-ending firework show illuminates the joy at hand. When we can't see the fireworks, we must switch our lens.

Let's be intentional in looking for hope.

Katherine Wolf is a rock-star lady who miraculously survived a catastrophic stroke after giving birth to her first son in 2008. She and her husband, Jay, have used every day since that life-changing event to speak life and hope into the broken hearts of others. This lovely and wise woman once described hope as the mingling of joy and sorrow.[13]

I love that so much. And not just because I love a good party and the opportunity to mingle with others.

Even when we walk faithfully with Jesus in our lives, hurtful and sorry things happen to us, all while paralleled with good and happy. Thankfully, Jesus equals hope! He is the solution to our life struggles of joy and sorrow intermingled.

We don't need to give the pain in our life the upper hand. In the same breath, we shouldn't allow pride to dissolve the bouts of stretching and strengthening that we're enduring from within.

Soaring trumpets filled the sanctuary with celebratory praise of our risen Savior one Easter morning. Lights were bright and worshippers' hands held high in surrender and gratitude to the One who beat death and paved a way for us on that third day following His crucifixion.

As I looked to my side to gaze at our "sorority" in their matching linen dresses, my heart raced a bit as I stood awestruck of the three blessings of swaying, singing sisters that stood between Austin and me.

My eyes tracked back to the choir, and my heart that had been racing seconds before was now paused in a flutter as I noticed the family that was occupying the pew in front of us.

I had not noticed them upon our entering the sanctuary because our punctuality on Sundays is spotty (Satan really works to ignite some Sunday morning fires within our house as we prepare to leave for fellowship with other believers). This Easter morning was no different, as we arrived during the second song and hurriedly shooed our line of ducklings up the steps to our beloved nosebleed section of the sanctuary.

The precious family that sent my heart into an arrhythmia outwardly appeared courageous. Less than six months before, this awestriking crew had to say goodbye to their wife and mother, after a hard-fought battle against cancer.

This lady was a woman of faith who was involved and respected throughout the community. For Pete's sake, she was a mother of twins, so I know she had to be tough as nails under her warm smile and words of grace and wisdom that she extended freely to all.

I saw her children standing with their eyes closed and hands raised as they worshipped. Her husband stood between a son and daughter, but his lips weren't moving. I could see the tears that were welling up in his eyes. He appeared to be caught in a heart storm of joy and pain.

His presence alone showed his obedience, praise, and joy, for his Savior.

His still lips were a clue of the pain stirring within.

I watched him and vividly remembered the early days of grieving our babies that are in heaven. Some days it was impossible to verbally release words of praise and God's goodness. I may have believed wholeheartedly in God's sovereignty and faithfulness, but the combination of lyrics and music would cause my lips to tremble and the floodgates to open at any moment.

God doesn't condemn us for paralyzed lips. His grace is sufficient for us all.

Though this family had fresh, fresh wounds of emptiness, shock, and grief, the strength of the Lord was displayed through their decision to show up. They were each on different wave lengths in displaying praise, but all in all, they were present.

We've all experienced some sort of heartache like this family. A situation left us with despair and longing for someone that is no longer reachable on planet earth. Through our personal sadness, what remains constant is the choice to switch our current perspective and the choice to be present in life.

At times, the joy and pain that race throughout our minds and bodies simultaneously make us feel one sentence away from being the newest character in *One Flew Over the Cuckoo's Nest.*

But guess what?

You're a child God loves and cherishes. A chosen son or daughter of the One who created you and desires for you to experience joy for eternity.

Let's remember that life's trials and triumphs will peel off like an Olympian's suit and accessories after the synchronized swimming event. But an eternal joy of Jesus Christ is unremovable and will remain forever.

You're still swimming in your event. The burning pains and breathless moments may be coming in more frequent and profound waves, but you're still present.

Keep wowing yourself and the world with persistence in your life's synchronized swim routine. Regardless of what sensations and unknowns arise and leave you feeling a flood of emotions, the joy of the Lord is your strength. Nehemiah 8:10 tells us so.

And always remember that the medic who is poolside to our lives' Olympic events is Jesus Christ. He will dive to the greatest depths to save and rescue us. He also walks on water, so when we're gasping for air and struggling to make our next move, there's no need that is out of His saving reach.

Check It

1: Can you think of a particular season in life when you were holding joy and pain in the same hand? Can you see God's presence threaded throughout that season?

2: Read Nehemiah 8:10 three times. Fully absorb the profoundness of its words—"the joy of the LORD is your strength" (CSB). Jesus finds such joy in *you*! His love for you that overspills into joy is then the fueling strength to help you move forward in good or bad times.

Affirmation (Come on, sister! Say it loud! Say it proud!)

God, you are with me here.

God, you were with me there.

God, you are with me everywhere in my life.

Through the happy and the hurt, *you are with me*,
and you love me without end.

I'm claiming and acting on these words in
Psalm 77:11–14 (ESV), "I will remember the deeds
of the Lord; yes, I will remember your wonders of
old. I will ponder all your work, and meditate on
your mighty deeds. Your way, O God, is holy.
What god is great like our God? You are the God
who works wonders . . ."

Lenses of Love

IF YOU'RE A COLLEGE FOOTBALL FAN, THEN YOU HAVE LIKELY heard the name of legendary walk-on player Brandon Burlsworth. Before finishing his collegiate career as an All-American, Brandon played for the Arkansas Razorbacks.

Wooooo Pig Soiee!

Wearing his iconic black, horn-rimmed eyeglasses while on and off the field, Brandon possessed a work ethic unlike any other. Those glasses of a gentle giant represented generosity, love, determination, and benevolence.

Brandon modeled the idea of anything is possible when you put your mind to it. He was the first Razorback to complete his master's degree before playing his final football game.[14]

Brandon was highly successful, driven, and hard working.

Though a recruited, redshirt freshman, Brandon was determined to do whatever it took to be exceptional. After a freshman year of strict dieting and rigorous workout routines, Brandon's muscle weight amplified, and his skillful footwork continued to leave others amazed at what a six-foot-three man could dance. After an entire year of working tirelessly both inside and outside of the classroom, Brandon received a scholarship.

He was a man of rooted faith, despite the challenges that encompassed his life as a child and through his college years. His persistence and dedication to his vision for his dream was stronger than those challenges. His character made him a dominant player.

Then . . . April 28, 1999.

Less than two weeks after being drafted by the National Football League's Indianapolis Colts, twenty-two-year-old Brandon traveled to his hometown to attend church with his mom. His journey home to see his momma was cut short. Brandon died in a car crash.

Tragedy.

Heart stopping and heart stomping. That's what it felt like as an Arkansan on that April day.

I recall the somber faces of local television announcers as they reported the news and tremendous loss to our state.

Draped over my parents' blue porcelain bathtub were newspaper articles that read, "Colts' pick killed in crash" and described how deeply Arkansans were affected by Brandon's passing.

Here in "the Natural State," we occasionally practice our earthquake drills because the New Madrid fault line could crank out some shakes at any point. However, in my lifetime we've never experienced an intense earthquake.

The day that Brandon passed away was the closest thing I can remember to any earthshaking occurrence at that point in my growing up years. We were living our lives and feeling some forward momentum, grateful to watch a young man find success.

Then, *boom!* It all seemingly crumbled and broke.

We have all heard stories that increase our heart rate as we think of the triumph and conquering that people have encountered. Our inward being leaps for joy at the success of someone we may not even know. Yet only a sentence later, we're left holding our breath as our eyes scan words of catastrophe. Our hearts can't grasp or fathom the hurt and intensity that a family and circle of friends are left to live in, day in and day out on this earth.

In Brandon's case, his family, friends, and fellow Razorbacks made the decision to shape good from their grief-stricken reality. Their perspective is clearly focused on bettering the lives of others—while honoring the life and legacy through the Brandon Burlsworth Foundation.

Even Brandon's glasses style was a walk-on. Eyes of a Champion is a program within Brandon's foundation that provides free eye exams and eyeglasses to children whose families are financially unable to provide proper eye care and assistance.

Once he knew that he was headed to the NFL, Brandon wanted to create space for underprivileged children to get the chance to experience a Razorback game day. Since the year 2000, during each football home game for the Arkansas Razorbacks, a section of bleachers is reserved for a special group of kiddos, welcomed over the stadium speakers as "the Burls Kids." After getting a tour of the stadium and walking on the field in their

Burls Kids jerseys, wearing their glasses that look like those worn by Brandon himself, the Burls Kids have front row seats and all the football snacks needed for a pig sooie shindig.

Don't stories like these leave us trying to make heads or tails of a situation? We wonder how so much hard-earned success could be paused in an instant. I'm constantly reminded that God doesn't add the same way we do. There is no definitive Excel spreadsheet or exact rationale. Austin reminded me of this one post-soccer practice evening when we were reviewing multiplication word problems with our twins, Emmie and Atalie. The sisters and I were in need of some WD-40 for our brains—we just weren't computing the numbers into the places they were supposed to go. (That's right, me included. A college graduate with a bachelor's degree was riding the third-grade math struggle bus.) As the girls and I shook our heads in confusion, Austin, our household math whiz, stated, "Math is black and white—it's facts. Math has no room for emotion."

Boy, am I thankful that God's math is more graciously creative and vast than academic math:

- Casualty and tremendous loss = Brandon's life ended tragically at a young age, when it seemed his professional success was on its way to exponential growth.

- Gain of goodness in the wake of grief = twenty-plus years of physical and emotional support for countless children, in particularly for those with limited opportunities.

The playing field is the same for us all.

We all endure loss. How we perceive our gains and losses is a conscious and constant decision for us individually.

In June of 2017, Austin and I had another shift of perspective in life. We viewed our growing family in the light of surprised and excited anticipation—we were pregnant with our third daughter. However, our journey took a lousy twist and we found ourselves breathless and face down in a trench.

We all end up in these wretched ditches. Life's road map has countless intersections of hurt and heartache, as we venture toward our destination.

Austin and I left our obstetrician's office with an ultrasound picture in hand of a perfectly healthy-looking profile of our baby girl. But she was lifeless. Her heartbeat had stopped a few days earlier.

We had to go home to our toddlers, Atalie and Emmie, who were so eager to meet their baby, Ruth. The girls that we had to face and deliver such devastating, life-changing news to were the same faces that were beaming with pride and excitement at the last ultrasound during which they saw Ruth wiggling around and "waving" to them.

Austin and I knew that we wanted to protect Atalie and Emmie's hearts from hurt as much as we possibly could, yet *it's through the wrestling and seeking that we learn and grow immensely in life.* They merit the truth. Our girls had the right to cry, to get angry, and to feel all their own feels upon hearing that they would not be able to hold their baby Ruth here on earth.

After getting our own emotions in check and somewhat under control, Austin and I tenderly and openly explained that baby Ruth was now in heaven.

Their immediate responses were along the lines of "No, I want my baby back!" However, a light bulb rapidly turned on in their minds. "So, baby Ruth is in heaven with Mom?"

It was a breathtaking moment. Austin and I sat there in disbelief at how many dots were connecting and coming full circle in their almost three-year-old minds.

"Mom," not to be confused with "Momma," was my grandmother who'd passed away the year before. The first time Austin listened to me tell a story about my grandmother when we were dating was one for the books. As I was talking about Mom, Austin tried to follow along respectfully the best he could with the information I was relaying. Bless him. I could tell something wasn't lining up in his brain. He eventually broke down and said with a puzzled look, "Are you telling me that you call your grandmother Mom and your mom, Mom?"

"Ha-ha! Of course not," I replied. "I call my grandmother Mom and my mother is Momma."

I don't know if Austin smelled something distasteful or if he was about to sneeze, but the look on his face following my explanation was enigmatic.

Now, back to Mom. My *grandmother*.

Atalie and Emmie were only twenty months old when we began those repeated conversations surrounding the idea of "Mom is in heaven with God and Jesus—and with Jesus as our Savior and the boss of our lives, we can see Mom again one day in heaven too!"

As hurtful as it is to lose loved ones, a bridge of opportunity is constructed between this temporary world we live in, to the eternal lifetime that is to come, if we choose to see the situation with a gospel worldview.

I treasure memories of Atalie and Emmie swinging in our backyard with their eyes gazing into the clear blue sky up above as they pumped their little legs back and forth, while their hair swayed and bounced with each back-and-forth motion. We do a lot of rabbit-chasing thinking in our house. Our twins included. Playground conversation would go from a five-minute discussion on which animals live in the trees followed by the pondering of whether or not squirrels like to eat flowers for snacks along with their acorns. I love it. And then to keep me on my toes, they throw out comments like "So Mom is out there in heaven with God and Jesus?" in mid-squirrel sentence. From animal habitats to squirrel appetites to heaven, we keep conversation lively and genuine at the White house.

Atalie and Emmie were entranced with the reality of heaven following my grandmother's death. They talked about it all the time, asking questions, and repeating the same facts over and over, again. They wanted to fully grasp it. And praise God the Holy Spirit stirred within their young hearts until they got it.

As our girls later suffered through the unforeseen loss of their grandfather, almost one year to the day after losing baby Ruth, the heaven reality became more and more desiring and real.

From a wildly young age, our twins have been encompassed in the emotions, hurt, and physical emptiness of loss. They entirely comprehend the reality of loss. And through it all they've asked the hard questions, cried the tears, made the snarky statements, but have believed in God and heaven with the remarkable faith of a child.

I want to be just like them.

This whole reality of life being cumbersome and unkind has pulled my naïve, fairytale-loving self out of the clouds, and planted my feet back here on planet earth. Gravity's role has magnified in my understanding throughout the last decade.

The sisters piled into the car after a half day of kindergarten. Second semester into the school year, I had finally grasped the mom wisdom of not trying to have a conversation with our children until after I fed them. Free mom advice from one who learned the hard way and took way too long to understand: whether your kiddos go a half or full day to school, smile and toss a Ziploc with a turkey sausage link, string cheese, and saltines to the lions in the back of your car. The balancing of their blood sugar tames their emotions.

After listening to some music in silence while the girls inhaled their snacks, I led with my typical, "How was your day, sisters?"

Our Little Bit, Atalie, was the first to chime in. (Side note: we call her Little Bit because she was a hair over the four-pound mark when we brought her and her twin sister home as babies. Healthy as a horse but as tiny as a Yorkie pup.)

"Good. We played octoball at recess. Elizabeth had goldfish at snack too! *Hmm*, we prayed for Ben's sister during prayer time. Hey, can I order lunch on Wednesday? Oh, and I asked Jesus to be boss of my life today."

Say *what*?

My momma heart was ecstatic. I quickly detoured the car to head to Austin's office so we could share the big news with him.

Turns out, Atalie was in STEM class praying on her own while her teacher was leading the class in a prayer. But hey, when the Holy Spirit moves, you've got to follow. Even if that means filtering out the prayer of someone else.

Fast-forward three months and our Emmie bug, Atalie's twin sister, came running to me at school pickup with arms wide open. She buried her dreamy curly-headed self into my stomach. With a humble but excited sparkle from her eyes and smile Emmie said, "Mommy, today in PE I asked Jesus to be the boss of my life."

Whoop! Whoop! Such a praise!

As Emmie tells it, she was receiving her daily instruction in PE class when she had the talk with Jesus about her need for a savior. Again, when the Holy Spirit moves, you act. Even if it drowns out the rules for sharks and minnows.

Through trauma, depths of heartbreak, and amidst turbulent feelings, each step of our struggle can frame a staircase to good and victory.

- Casualty and tremendous loss = Our Atalie and Emmie suffered the loss of a great-grandmother, baby sister, and grandfather.

- Gain of goodness in the wake of grief = Eternal salvation for our sisters. (Cue the tears.) God used every thought and question the girls had through those losses, and He drew their hearts to Him. They have secured their eternity in heaven as they recognized the size and might of the God who knows the number of days and years to each of our lives!

Again, God's math doesn't always seem the clearest in our minds. It can take years of looking for the missing pieces of the equation and then intentionally laying out all the pieces to form an equation and come up with a sum:

For example, 25 + 25 = 50.

So does 40 + 10, 30 + 20, and 5 + 45. And the possibilities go on.

God gives us all different addends, or scenarios, to work with in life.

God got ahold of our girls' hearts at a very early age. They've done their fair share of sifting and sorting through stories and hard questions in the Bible. And not by any award-winning parenting on mine and Austin's end but by the goodness of the God who reaches out to us. My honey and I have encountered countless parenting moments of side-eyeing each other when the sisters tag team us with statements like, "Jesus was God, but Jesus is God's son?" or "The Holy Spirit is God, too, so how are three people actually just one person?'" Thank you for the reminders, sisters! There are concepts and depths of the gospel that are difficult even for adults to fully process and explain. Yet when we can't answer a question directly, Austin and I have no problem saying, "You know what, we need to look that up together—mommies and daddies learn every day, just like you!"

Understanding the life cycle of a butterfly or quantum mechanics requires exercise of the brain.

Understanding emotional and spiritual issues calls for exercise of the heart. Our posture to listen and learn is a crucial component in receiving information and gaining newfound perspective.

We can help each other in the math equations of life and remember that God's ways are not our ways. Sometimes one person's life-changing event can lead to another life-changing event in the lives of others, just like the case of Brandon Burlsworth and the loss of my grandmother, my daddy, and our baby Ruth.

God can be glorified through our brokenness.

Check It

1: What is an example in your life where God's math left you in awe and wonder?

2: Think back to one of the most difficult seasons you have encountered in life up to this point. Now fast-forward to where you are today. In between those two dots on your life's timeline, can you see a gain of goodness in the wake of your difficulty?

Affirmation (Come on, sister! Say it loud! Say it proud!)

God, you are with me here.

God, you were with me there.

God, you are with me everywhere in my life.

Through the happy and the hurt, *you are with me,*
and you love me without end.

I'm claiming and acting on these words in
Psalm 77:11–14 (ESV), "I will remember the deeds
of the Lord; yes, I will remember your wonders of
old. I will ponder all your work, and meditate on
your mighty deeds. Your way, O God, is holy.
What god is great like our God? You are the God
who works wonders . . ."

Option A and B

I LOVE THIS VERSE IN THE OLD TESTAMENT. ECCLESIASTES 7:14 (ESV) tells us, "In the day of prosperity be joyful, and in the day of adversity consider: God has made the one as well as the other."

Boy, do I need this reminder on the daily to keep my perspective centered on Christ.

In a whirlwind moment of mayhem, I can quickly lose all grasp of the gospel worldview that I should look through 24–7.

But the truth is undeniable. The same God who sits on the throne when we're enjoying life is the same God who sits on the throne when the world around us seems to disintegrate.

God is constant in our lives and He's not only worthy of praise during the good times, but in the yucky times as well. Whether we have the correct perspective in the moment is detrimental to our present circumstance and future. Perspective checks are a big honkin' deal!

We must learn to focus more clearly when wading through the wave pool of life. Waves of all sorts come barreling towards us. Disappointment, unworthiness, shame, despair, ambition, excitement, surprised, tragedy and loss—they're all an unknown wavelength away from slamming us.

So let's work on our focus.

"Mrs. White," said the green scrub-wearing lady from the doorway.

I stood up with all my belongings in tow. While walking toward her, I was startled by a growling sound to my right. I jumped in shock but turned to find that it was just Mr. Henry snoring from his waiting room chair. Oh, to be able to find such relaxation and rest in a doctor's office.

"Good afternoon. Follow me this way. You're here for your annual checkup, Mrs. White?"

"Yes, ma'am."

"Wonderful. Have a seat right here and the doctor will be with you shortly."

The doctor came in a few minutes later and we chatted about how much our kiddos were growing and all the momma-heart-feels that come with that. Then she pulled the enormous machine in front of my face. That *phoropter*, as the professionals call it, is an impressive piece of machinery.

I scooched forward and situated my eyes behind the lenses.

"When you read this line of letters, is option A or option B clearer?" the doctor asked as she clicked the lens back and forth.

Sometimes the choices are vastly different and easy to decipher. Other times, I find myself really squinting and having to ask her to go back to the first option because the difference between the two really wasn't very clear to me.

More and more, I realize that I'm checking my daily perspective of life in that same manner. Through those clicks of life's phoropter, I've been able to find that even in the messiest and hardest instances, God is there.

I've learned from Deuteronomy 4:29 (CSB) how pertinent it is for me to wholeheartedly do the work of finding God—for me to sit behind my life's phoropter and intentionally click through the different lenses of grace, forgiveness, understanding, patience, and hope. "But from there, you will search for the LORD your God, and you will find him when you seek him with all your heart and all your soul." And so I've engrained that truth of scripture into my heart and mind. It doesn't say that we might encounter God. It says *we will*. We will find Him when we've searched with all our heart and all our soul.

God is in option A and option B. Always.

"I will never leave you nor forsake you," Hebrews 13:5 (ESV). That sure sounds like a lovely phrase. However, as we absorb the weight and brokenness of this world we live in, we can be left questioning the promise of Hebrews 13.

Sometimes, we place blame on God for the hurts and hardships in our lives. Other times we tell ourselves that He is simply silent and absent.

But He's not.

Hurtful and immature words or actions can leave our friendships in pieces on the floor like a puzzle at a sleepover that got trampled on by the crowd running to popcorn and a movie.

Irrational deals and dishonest people can lead to financial trauma that leaves us suffering and trying to get out of a well of debt for years.

An MRI reveals hot spots showing that the cancer returned, and we assume that healing may never come to us again.

Where is this never-leaving, never-forsaking God in all the daunting accounts of our lives?

Maybe the question should be, "Where is our perspective?" Are we viewing our circumstance through a gospel-centered lens?

Have we turned the knob on our life's phoropter so we can clearly see the hope and love that pushes us forward, while vividly seeing and acknowledging the God that's beside us throughout all of life's conflicts and celebrations?

As we migrate through life together, let's encourage one another to check our lenses of perspective regularly.

It's OK to click back and forth between option A and B to help us sift and sort through our heart's and mind's view. Regardless which lens we settle on, we are never alone! While our human minds must make choices, our God has only one viewpoint.

A lens of perfect love that is unchanging.

There's no human view too out of focus for Jesus's grace and love to make clear.

Check It

1: Right now, in this moment, are you struggling to see God's presence in your life? Clean off any guilt, grudges, or greed from your conscience. Now, click through your current circumstances with the lenses of hope, love, forgiveness, and so on. Do you see Him now? Give yourself grace and time in this process. Because the God who is undoubtedly present is patiently beside you in your pondering.

2: Do you know a friend or loved one who is currently trying to catch a breath as they swim in heartache? That heartache can be from actual loss of a loved one, flopped finances, trauma from an affair, or deep depression from Satan's antics in their mind. Wearing your lenses of love, run to them with listening ears and open arms. Speak life and encouragement to them at volumes that rattle windows!

Affirmation (Come on, sister! Say it loud! Say it proud!)

God, you are with me here.

God, you were with me there.

God, you are with me everywhere in my life.

Through the happy and the hurt, *you are with me,*
and you love me without end.

I'm claiming and acting on these words in Psalm 77:11–14 (ESV), "I will remember the deeds of the Lord; yes, I will remember your wonders of old. I will ponder all your work, and meditate on your mighty deeds. Your way, O God, is holy. What god is great like our God? You are the God who works wonders . . ."

PART 3

Painful Enhancements . . .
With a Present God

A Stalled Shark

OOKS LIKE YOU FOUND YOURSELF SOME HOMESCHOOL-ing items," said the friendly lady from behind the plexiglass barrier at Mardel's register one. (COVID, you've proven to be a divider on a lot of levels in our transitioning society, but we're still going to do life well and *with* others despite your forced impediments.)

"Oh, yes, ma'am. I'm a total newbie to this world of homeschooling. I'm working to get my dining room-turned-classroom ready for our year to begin. We're just waiting for all of our curriculum to come in." Truth be told, I probably didn't need the neon-colored WikkiStix on my school supply list, but I let them slide right over the scanner between the continents map and purple organizing bins.

As I was exiting the building to head back to my mom-wagon, I heard a strong bass bumping whose volume was increasing. It was a deep thumping beat you could feel vibrate within your chest, even though you might be thirty yards away from the sound source. I stopped to look both ways.

The car cruised by at the pace of a gangster on the prowl. Then I heard the brief lyrics of the song jolting through the speakers, out the car windows, and echoing through the shopping center: "You're not swimming with sharks, you're a guppy."

I smiled and chuckled like an immature schoolgirl as I tried to translate how that play on words could be applied to my life. The only reference I had for guppy was when Ariel called Flounder a guppy, or a scaredy fish, in the movie *The Little Mermaid*. But come on, y'all know I got too distracted by the beat of the song—my south Arkansas fibers were starting to vibrate and I was just trying not to show my "stanky leg" right there at the crosswalk in front of the Christian bookstore.

"You're not swimming with sharks, you're a guppy." I mentally repeated the song's lyrics three or four more times. Though I've yet to figure out why I'm the guppy in this scenario, the term *shark* did trigger my brain.

I had recently brushed up on my children's latest issue of *Ranger Rick Jr.* while in between loads of laundry on the couch. A caption that read something along the lines of *some sharks must move forward in order to breathe* caught my scatterbrained attention.

Was Ranger Rick pulling my leg? Is that true that some sharks will literally die if they're still? I needed to know more.

Turns out, Ranger Rick was *right*. Some sharks do require movement to live.

Per the Google, out of the four hundred species of sharks in our world, there are about two dozen species who require forward motion in order to breathe. A fancy science term for this type of shark is *obligate ram ventilator*.

I'm sure you're familiar with a couple of these huge fish. Great whites, hammerheads, and whale sharks all fall into the category of required, continuous swimming in order to maintain their water/blood gas exchange.

In layman's terms, great white sharks must swim with their mouths open at all times so oxygen-rich water can ram into their throats and through their gills, which equals breath and life. If these obligate ram ventilators stop moving to rest on the ocean floor like some of their cousin sharks, they will indeed drown and die.

Oh, and if you're wondering how a critter like the hammerhead shark can swim nonstop without rest, I'll go ahead and let you in on a little more insight. There is belief that a shark's swimming motion is coordinated by its spinal cord, not its brain. Therefore, the spinal cord can continue the shark in a forward, oxygen supplying motion, while its brain rests. If the shark aligns itself against a good, strong current, even better!

Isn't that incredible? Creation and science continue to rock my world in the best way. The God who created your very life created this mammoth of a predator with great precision, as well.

His greatness and creativeness is off the charts, my friends.

(And can I just say how thankful I am to be a human with a true sleeping cycle that allows me to *stop* and cuddle up in a still current within the covers of my bed?)

Again, I digress.

Thanks to the eye-opening of Ranger Rick, I can't help but think of us humans in the context of moving and living sharks.

When our relationship with family is on the rocks, or the boss won't stop micromanaging us despite our high performance, it's easy and natural for us to skitter away into isolation.

For some of us that looks like staying in bed for days to binge-watch Netflix behind bowls of salsa or leftover Halloween candy. There are others who would rather sleep away the pain and struggles of reality, falsely thinking that once we wake up, our problems will have vanished during our deep REM cycles.

Meanwhile, some of us choose to go about our daily routines like high functioning robots who are ignoring all incoming texts/calls/engagement from friends and family. We self-construct walls of separation.

If we stay still and alone, we can become paralyzed and forget to breathe—essentially, we're a stalled hammerhead shark at the ocean floor and we're drowning from our lack of forward motion. But our livelihood requires movement among community with others!

I say all this but y'all, I've done it. Heck, I still do it. Even though I know that community is life-giving and part of God's purpose in our lives, at times I continue to make isolating choices in self-defense during hurtful and stressful seasons.

But God. God has shown me the power of connectivity on many occasions, yet the instance that shines the brightest was one of literal life or death in my own life.

As I've mentioned before, in 2017, Austin and I lost our child, Ruth Michelle, through our third miscarriage.

Unlike our previous miscarriages, this time, my body didn't contract and naturally miscarry our eleven-week-old fetus, Ruth, who no longer had a heartbeat.

I took a round of medication that was supposed to induce contractions to begin the miscarrying process. However, the pill popping produced *zero* bent-over-the-knees-in-pain kind of contractions that I had experienced years prior.

As I sit here typing this out, each sentence sounds so cold and lifeless. The medical terms for it all are popping up in my nurse brain as I look for the words to describe this event and dang it if they don't sound awful too.

I hate it. And *I'm here with you* as you sit and think of your life happenings that are so hurtful and have left you with a jaw trembling in confusion and shatteredness. Unfortunately, we all have instances of harsh realities that are banked inside our souls and minds. But remember, we're doing some self-directed neuroplasticity. We're rewiring our brains as we think back over these times. And we're wiring in new narratives and pathways to these happenings that reveal God's presence with us *because He was.*

Friends, this is not a light and happy part of the journey.

We all have them.

It's the stuff no one enjoys talking about but once we do, God starts to reveal healing for us and for others through the tears and switching of our lenses as we reexamine the situation.

After several appointments of seeing Ruth's perfect profile on ultrasound, yet stillness from what should be a flickering heartbeat from her heart, Austin and I had to make the heart wrenching decision to have a D&C. With Ruth being larger than our first two babies at her time of passing, the miscarriage process was going to entail more physically.

Let's talk about conflicting faith. Austin and I made the decision to remove a lifeless human from my body, while fully believing in the God who historically raised people from the dead and we still believe that He works miracles today.

It was the hardest decision we had ever made in our married life.

We prayed countless, quivering words for guidance and clarity.

On June ninth, I was wheeled into a cold operating room with a baby in my belly. No, she didn't have a heartbeat, but I knew her body was there. Another life that had once shared life with me through a physical and heartful connection was being removed. A literal piece of my once livelihood was leaving me. A couple of hours later, I woke up in a frigid and dimly lit recovery room with my Austin holding my hand and leaning over the siderails with a look of broken love on his face.

There was no longer a baby in my body.

Austin felt the barrenness as much as I did.

I entered a time of questioning and nagging with God. I carried to Him all kinds of attitude and anger. Yet—as He always proves to be—God was so patient with me. With every question and sassy remark I spouted off, I sensed nothing but an (at the time irritating) extension of love from Him.

Can you relate? Haven't we all ventured through hardships and letdowns that landed us at the feet of the God of the universe to probe and doubt?

For weeks, I had postoperative spotting. The quantity of blood seemed to fall within the normal range of what to expect for the time frame we were in, but when the bleeding persisted for over a month and a half following my procedure, we needed to investigate further.

Turns out what we thought was a complete D&C was not. An ultrasound revealed that something foreign remained in my uterus. The piece of tissue left inside me was now increasing my risk of infection and hemorrhaging with each passing day.

Not only were Austin and I trying to wrestle through our own grief of Ruth, we were tenderly trying to remind Atalie and Emmie that God is a good and kind God, even though He willed for our baby to be in heaven instead of with us on earth. But now we had to further endure physical risks and trauma from an incomplete D&C? Really, God—are the wounds not raw enough? Let's just keep on sprinkling some salt into the exposed emotions and flesh of our hearts.

My OB-GYN prescribed me, yet again, another round of medication that should have induced contractions, in hopes of flushing out the tissue remaining.

Nada. No cramping, no increased spotting. Nothing.

Austin and I decided that our hearts needed a change of scenery in the doctor world. Maybe a fresh start and new perspective driving this ship would benefit us.

We called our fertility specialist from years before, and he graciously took us into his care. After all, once we finished addressing the incomplete D&C, he would likely need to help reset and manage my out-of-balance hormones, so we were thrilled to be under his wing again.

(In my hindsight vision, I can now see that this step in our story was a *game-changing* play in God's game calling on my life.)

As Austin and I sat across the desk in an eight-by-ten office space, our doctor made it very clear that he would allow us one more round of the contraction-inducing medication, but he wanted to eliminate this leftover tissue from my body at once.

He handed us a blue prescription paper. "You take this medication as written, but you call me in five days. If your body has not passed the remaining tissue, we will schedule surgery immediately. Your risk of bleeding and infection is becoming greater. If you pass the remains at home, I want you to take this cup and use it to bring me the tissue."

We took the brown paper bag like those that are scattered in the seats of a school bus carrying kiddos on a field trip. I wish it had been a lunch sack. Instead, this brown sack held a specimen cup for us to bring back remnants of a life that never lived outside of my womb.

I mustered up a grin as we pushed back our chairs and headed for the exit door. "Yes, sir. Thank you so much for taking care of us."

Austin and I were somewhat relieved that we were able to avoid a surgery at this time but also a bit uneasy of my being home alone with our "threenagers" and the possibility of bleeding out occurring. We voiced our concerns and needs to God as we traveled to the pharmacy to give this medication another shot.

Check It

1: Do you ever self-isolate when you start to feel overwhelmed by burdens and brokenness? Make a list of three people that you can call or text when you realize that you have a hammer in hand and are starting to build your isolation wall. These friends/family members are crucial to us moving forward.

2: If you're having one of those no-good-very-bad days and you can't think of a single person that you could call or text to confide in, write this down. *God.* Open a Bible. Google Bible verses on your phone or a library computer. Step outside and look at the world around you—the rocks, trees, birds flying, or landform encompassing you. Science didn't speak those things into existence. But the God who loves you did. And He's the God who is with you and reaching out for you when no other human in this world can ease your pain of loneliness.

Affirmation (Come on, sister! Say it loud! Say it proud!)

God, you are with me here.

God, you were with me there.

God, you are with me everywhere in my life.

Through the happy and the hurt, *you are with me,* and you love me without end.

I'm claiming and acting on these words in Psalm 77:11–14 (ESV), "I will remember the deeds of the Lord; yes, I will remember your wonders of old. I will ponder all your work, and meditate on your mighty deeds. Your way, O God, is holy. What god is great like our God? You are the God who works wonders . . ."

Worst-Case Scenario

MY D&C WAS IN JUNE 2017. AT THIS POINT IN THE GAME, IT was a sweltering, August day.

Atalie and Emmie were scheduled to start their first day of dance class in the days ahead, so our first stop of the morning was to a local dance store to purchase their first pairs of tap and ballet shoes.

Turns out, threenagers aren't always happy to stay on task, so my dreamy vision of shoe and leotard shopping landed me and the sisters back in the mom-wagon with heightened blood pressure and a new agenda after an insane shopping fiasco. We headed on down the road to Hobby Lobby.

Felt. We needed felt.

It was crucial that we gathered felt squares of all colors because our little trio was going to be completing a fruits of the Spirit lesson before the day turned to night. (Or so I thought.)

God heard my raging prayers of *Help!* as the curly-headed sisters in the back seat flipped their switches and started singing "I love you, Lord" with the most angelic looks on their faces.

Sheesh. Child-rearing can feel like an all-out juggling act of bipolar individuals (parents and kiddos alike) requiring extreme grace. My momma heart was in serious need of our fruits of the Spirit lesson. I was unquestionably falling short on some patience, kindness, and self-control.

After feeding the sweet minions and putting them down for a much-needed nap, I lit my favorite fall candle in the kitchen and grabbed our Hobby Lobby goods from the car. I plopped myself down on the carpet in our master bedroom with scissors and felt in hand.

The house was peaceful and quiet as the sisters sawed logs in their sleep from across the house. The essence of autumn filled our home and lowered my heart rate with each whiff that I took in.

I reached for my phone to call my honey, but quickly remembered that Austin was about forty-five minutes away at a real estate continuing education class. I settled for making mental notes on what our next conversation should entail.

As I started to cut out the green felt to bring to life our "pear for patience" fruit, my phone rang.

It was one of my mentors, Cita, whom I adore and would sit at the feet of for hours on end. Her sass, wisdom, and love for the Lord makes my heart swell with amazement. Cita was checking in on me, as she knew of the continued issues we were having from the incomplete D&C.

Since we can speak a salty narrative well with one another, I shared a dramatic, play-by-play of the morning that had landed me on the carpet cutting out shapes for the fruit of the Spirit.

In an instant, I felt a gush of blood.

"Hey, I think my body is finally passing this leftover tissue. Let me call you right back, OK?"

"Well, good! Yeah, just give me a call back and let me know if I can help."

I was walking toward the bathroom and remembered that our doctor wanted the tissue sample. "Actually, can you head on over here to sit with the sisters while they sleep? That way I can take this sample to the doctor's office. Austin won't be home until late tonight, and I should get this to the clinic today."

Without hesitation, Cita said, "I have my car keys in hand, and I'm headed out the door. I'll be there in about ten minutes."

"Wow. This is a lot of blood. Ummm, OK, yeah, I'm glad you're on your way. Because this is a lot. Of blood. See you in a bit." I was stuttering with worry now.

While in the bathroom trying to retrieve the plastic specimen cup from the brown lunch sack, I had this overwhelming feeling that what Austin and I had dreaded the possibility of—the worst-case scenario of my being home alone with toddlers in tow, hemorrhaging—was playing out.

Although Austin was in class, I felt like he would answer his phone, since this was arising unexpectedly and urgently, and he knew I wouldn't call otherwise.

The phone rang twice.

In a hushed and rapid voice, Austin answered. "Hey, is everything OK? We're in the middle of this course on legal contracts."

"Honey, I'm bleeding out and the blood isn't slowing down. Cita is on her way over, so I'm going to have her stay with the girls. I'll probably go ahead and drive to the hospital instead of the doctor's office with this sample," I said in a rushed panic.

In this moment of uncertainty and fear, I realized Austin was outside of the come-to-the-rescue zone for me. My parents were two hours away in my childhood hometown. My heart rate increased by ten beats with these realizations.

In the most tangible way, I felt my complete dependence on the Lord and my zero control over my own life and circumstances.

"I have to go, honey, this is a lot of blood. Oh my gosh. OK. Just meet me at the hospital. I love you."

Austin doesn't get too worked up over the what-ifs, but that guard was bulldozered down at this point. I could hear him closing books and jostling car keys as he said, "It's going to be OK, baby, I love you. I will see you there. Should I call an ambulance?"

I hung up the phone.

The chaos of the moment left me with no time.

Once I realized that this hemorrhaging was beyond a simple swoop of me catching some bloody specimen to deliver to the doctor's office, I realized my need for immediate help.

I stood up from my hunkered-over position in the bathroom and began walking to the kitchen to grab my car keys. After about five steps forward, I felt a heaviness in my chest and a ringing/fullness in my ears. I was incredibly lightheaded.

Oh no, I'm going to pass out, I thought.

Then I prayed, *God please keep me from passing out until I get the house door unlocked and the door open to the garage so someone can get inside this house to help me and take care of the girls.*

My prayer was answered.

I slapped the garage door opener on the wall and focused on trying to keep my eyes open. The dizziness and three o'clock afternoon sunshine were overcoming me with each rising inch of the garage door.

This is where I should tell you that our house was second from the end of a dead-end gravel road.

Sure, my nerves might have simmered a bit if I knew that I could fall out into the front yard of a high-traffic neighborhood where at least the Amazon driver might have noticed me passed out on the sidewalk, but this wasn't my reality. I was venturing out to slim pickins of help.

There was one neighbor who could see our driveway from theirs. But these friends both worked about thirty miles away from our road. Their children had graduated high school and were no longer at their house during daytime hours. My chances for seeing life beyond our gravel roundabout drive were few and far between.

The hum of the garage door motor fell silent as it was completely lifted.

I stopped and fell to my knees on the cool slab in our garage that met our gray rock drive.

In that moment, I felt like an obligate ram ventilating shark that had stopped.

Would my stillness and aloneness lead to death?

On that August day, I thought that my life was ending at thirty-one years of age.

If I continued to bleed out, it might be too late by the time Cita arrived at our house.

The blood continued in waves of all magnitudes.

The idea of driving myself to the hospital was a joke. I couldn't even keep my eyes open or stand up. It was all I could do to not hyperventilate from anxiety.

I guess I could call an ambulance to the house, but who knew how long it would take for them to arrive? The closest fire station was ten minutes away—and it was a *volunteer* station. Tack on the drive time for volunteers to arrive at the station, and my situation was growing darker with each passing thought.

I needed to get closer into town.

I needed to keep my perspective in check. And thankfully, God laid His hand on me.

Check It

1: Have you ever found yourself in a situation where you realized your complete lack of control, despite how organized, brilliant, physically capable, or driven you were?

2: After you think of that no-control moment, remember God's presence throughout that entire situation. What interventions of comfort did He provide?

Affirmation (Come on, sister! Say it loud! Say it proud!)

God, you are with me here.

God, you were with me there.

God, you are with me everywhere in my life.

Through the happy and the hurt, *you are with me*,
and you love me without end.

I'm claiming and acting on these words in
Psalm 77:11–14 (ESV), "I will remember the deeds
of the Lord; yes, I will remember your wonders of
old. I will ponder all your work, and meditate on
your mighty deeds. Your way, O God, is holy.
What god is great like our God? You are the God
who works wonders . . ."

Propelled by Community

between the people of Israel and their enemies from Amalek. (You can read about it in Exodus 17:8–16.) It gives us a strong perspective on God's constant presence for His people and the significance of doing life with others, especially in our times of weakness.

As Joshua and the Israelites faced the Amalek people on the battlefront, Moses (who was also Team Israelite) stood on the top of the hill to hold up the staff of God in his hands. Accompanying Moses were two men, Aaron and Hur:

> Whenever Moses held up his hand, Israel prevailed, and whenever he lowered his hand, Amalek prevailed. But Moses' hands grew weary, so they took a stone and put it under him, and he sat on it, while Aaron and Hur held up his hands, one on one side, and the other on the other side. So his hands were steady until the going down of the sun. And Joshua overwhelmed Amalek and his people with the sword." (Exodus 17:11–13 ESV)

Do you see it? Aaron and Hur stepped in and literally held up the hands of Moses in his moments of physical weakness and incapability. Through a display of community and God's constant presence, the Israelites defeated the army of Amalek.

What a picture of togetherness. Of doing life *with* others and doing *for* them when they themselves can't muster up the strength to keep going in a forward motion.

We engage in social and personal battles on all fronts. Life hits us hard with relationship tiffs, health declines, and paralyzing anxiety. We can find ourselves, like I did, as a hammerhead shark, motionless and drowning in the ocean of our life's stress.

There I was, bleeding on the floor of our garage. As I used every bit of control within my body, I looked up and over to the one neighbor's house within view.

Lo and behold, their garage door was open and, in my peripheral vision, I could see a waving blur. Our neighbor and friend, who worked for the state, just so happened to be home on a Wednesday afternoon at three o'clock and was waving to me from the end of his driveway. When Randy saw me flail my arm in the air as a pitiful excuse of a wave, he instantly knew something wasn't right and ran across to me.

"Randy, I'm bleeding a lot and I need to get to the hospital. My friend is almost here so she will be with the girls soon, but I need you to go get my car keys and blow out the candle on the kitchen counter," I said very matter-of-factly.

Randy did those exact things.

He also got me a towel to sit on in the car. Boy, was I thankful our dear friend and neighbor was a husband and girl dad. Between that assurance of his not being too alarmed by "girl stuff" and my no-filter-nurse-self, there was no room for shame as we turned up gravel in our rushed driving down the road.

"Did you blow out the kitchen candle?" I asked behind closed eyelids.

Even amongst all the physical trauma of me, I couldn't stop thinking about our girls at home with access to a burning flame. Toddlers know everything and know how to do everything . . . until they don't; hence my urgency to confirm the blowing out of the candle.

"I did. I sure did," Randy confirmed for me in a calm tone.

"We'll stop at the gas station on Lawson. I'm going to have an ambulance meet us there."

"Are you sure?" Randy asked. "I can get us all the way into town pretty quickly and straight to the hospital."

"No. I think this plan will work well because I need some fluids fast." Miraculously, in and out of thinking straight and borderline passing out, my nursing brain was computing blood loss = need for IV fluids, *stat*.

As I reclined in the passenger's seat with my feet elevated on the dashboard in hopes of getting some form of blood flow back to my head, I made the call to 911 and told them where we would be.

It doesn't even make sense how in this moment of limbo, anxiety, and bleeding, my brain was able to function at all. In hindsight, I can see that some well-paved, first aid neuropathways must have been very present and I was simply able to think on a well-established course of knowledge. God was interceding all the way to my brain waves. He was unfolding each passing moment with His might and timing—completely in control of it all.

He had placed me within community.

I was like Moses in the story of the Israelites and Amalek—I was literally unable to physically stand, but in came our friend and neighbor to hold me up and keep my battle for life in a victorious trajectory. My friend Cita was already selflessly en route to our home to sit with the twins.

As Randy put the car into park at the gas station, I tried to keep my eyes focused and looking straight ahead of me.

I began handing Randy my wedding rings and my grandmother's engagement ring that I wear daily. (How many times have you found yourself in a similar scenario? "Hey, lovely neighbor, I'm an embarrassed bleeding mess over here, but can you sit with me for ten minutes while you're driving my car? Oh, and here, I'm going to leave you with some of my most valuable and sentimental pieces of jewelry." Y'all, I've never collected a paycheck from Hollywood—but you can't make this stuff up in real life.)

We pulled into the gas station parking lot on four wheels, despite our "emergency speed limit."

"Thank you so much for getting me here, Randy." I could hear the siren of the ambulance growing closer. "Please put these rings in the glove box and we'll get them at home. I don't want to beat Austin to the hospital and have to trust that my rings are well taken care of. I need them in a safe spot."

"I'll do it. It's all going to be OK. You just lay right there until the ambulance parks," Randy ordered.

Slow, deep breaths, I kept repeating to myself. The paramedics and Randy assisted me and my bloody towel to the gurney.

Next thing I knew, I was simultaneously answering questions, watching the medic start an IV, and saying lots of prayers of thanks as we drove away from my momwagon at the gas station that sunny afternoon.

All I could do was pray.

"God, you're doing it all. I'm completely helpless here but you've surrounded me with people. You're keeping me alive. Thank you for loving me."

I no longer felt like I was drowning at the bottom of the ocean. I had found a current of community that was propelling me in a forward motion and allowing me to live and breathe.

That day I witnessed the profound and lifegiving power in friendships.

In case you're wondering, Cita arrived at our house about two minutes after Randy and I left. The road was still dusty from our spinouts when she pulled down the drive.

Also, Austin had called to let his mom know what was happening and she just so happened to be shopping in a town near our house, so she was able to go and help Cita with our Atalie and Emmie.

God is *amazing*! That's some beautiful unfolding in big uncertainty.

While Randy and I were handling the situation on the home front, Austin was ahead of the game, as he always is. God told him to call our fertility doctor to let him know what was going down.

Our doctor met me in the ER.

He performed my surgery that day. Through our years of working with him, Austin and I have always felt such peace in his care. His heartfelt bedside manner, continued dedication to hormonal women, and book knowledge landed him with a big ol' trust medal from our family.

While I was in the ER waiting on an operating room to become vacant, Ellen, one of our closest college friends who was a nurse practitioner at the hospital, came by to calm my heart with a hug and uplifting words of love.

I remember being wheeled to the OR and seeing a dear friend's husband, Ben, in the back hallway as he was leaving from his nurse anesthetist duties of the day.

He told me the name of his friend who would be administering my anesthesia during the surgery.

Our friends' words of comfort and faces of familiarity further anchored my heart in peace in a not so peaceful scenario.

Throughout that day, God displayed to me His power and plan for my life. He showed me that despite my everyday key family members' being displaced in my hour of great need, it wasn't a coincidence. God had strategically placed everyone in the right place, at the right time.

For me?

Yes and no.

Ultimately, this is all about God's glory being revealed. Our community served as instruments in God's saving of my thirty-one-year-old self.

Though I didn't complete *my* fruits of the Spirit lesson with our girls, *God* taught me and my family a magnified and way-more-powerful lesson on the fruits of the Spirit than any felt cutouts ever would have.

Family and friends poured out *love* on us.

Our hearts were fueled with *joy* as each piece of the puzzle connected.

The presence of community brought us *peace*.

My racing heart learned *patience*.

I could see *kindness* extended all around me.

The actions of servanthood displayed in our community radiated *goodness* into my weary soul.

As people showed up to help, my heart learned what absolute *faithfulness* looked like.

When my body felt like it had nothing else to give, I understood *gentleness* as others physically stepped into the gaps for me.

I watched Austin and my parents exhibit *self-control* as they wanted to come running in for my rescue, but God had set them in different locations in order for the power and goodness of community and God to be revealed.

My life has never been the same since that August day. Nicole Nordeman's lyrics to "Sound of Surviving" became my motto for that season of my life. Do yourself a favor and go check out that song. I wonder if the lyrics will resonate with a season of your life and we can share a song motto together?

A moment of chaos while alone was the start of a gift that God was giving me. He was revealing His ultimate control and compassion.

From it all, I was still living. The pain, the blood, the heartache, and fighting, were all strengthening me.

I'm forever thankful for the Aarons and Hurs in my life on that fear-filled day—and those who have loved and rescued me between my ages of zero and thirty-seven.

But I'll be the first to admit that I do occasionally sneak off to lay like a starfish in our master closet for a few moments of silence and solitude. Can I get an amen?

Sure, we all need our space at times. Jesus went away to be alone on many occasions throughout His life.

Yet community and surrounding Himself with others was also a feature of his life's story.

God in the flesh was born as a baby. He didn't enter this world as a grown man who was established and knew how to care for His every need. Nope! He came into the world dependent on others. Jesus's parents cared for His needs. He sat among leaders in the temple, where He listened, asked questions, and learned.

Let's also think about the day Jesus was crucified. After being brutally tortured and beaten, the Romans forced Jesus to carry the very cross that He would be nailed to. As you can imagine, Jesus's human body grew weak and unable to carry the one hundred–plus pound crossbeam of solid wood. This led to one of the Roman soldiers calling on a man from the crowd to finish carrying the cross up the hill for Jesus.

I once learned in a church sermon that there are only about fifty-two days of Jesus' life recorded in the Bible. Despite that small number, I've found that the bookends of His life stand as a remarkable display of leaning into the help and offerings of others. If God in the flesh could be found to thrive within community and with the help of others, shouldn't we?

Let's be the Aarons and Hurs who stand alongside our friends in their weak and dark hours. We can physically lend a helping hand, but when our pin is too far away from theirs on a map, we can always pray for them.

We need to be like Moses and allow others to help us when our hearts or bodies are growing weak. I completely understand the "Oh, I don't want to burden anyone else with my troubles" mentality, but I can tell you from hard lessons learned that that thought process is cheap and faulty.

If the Son of God can rely on and accept help from others, we sure better take a swig of some humble juice and allow others to reach out to us. Let's find our community and stay active in its current, so we don't end up like a stalled and lifeless shark.

Check It

1: Can you think of a time when your friends or family members stepped in to lift you up, just as Aaron and Hur did for Moses?

2: Are you connected in a community of believers? Maybe it's a small group at church or a group of friends in your neighborhood. Make sure you're being propelled by community.

Affirmation (Come on, sister! Say it loud! Say it proud!)

God, you are with me here.

God, you were with me there.

God, you are with me everywhere in my life.

Through the happy and the hurt, *you are with me,*
and you love me without end.

I'm claiming and acting on these words in
Psalm 77:11–14 (ESV), "I will remember the deeds
of the Lord; yes, I will remember your wonders of

old. I will ponder all your work, and meditate on your mighty deeds. Your way, O God, is holy. What god is great like our God? You are the God who works wonders . . ."

Where's the Playbook?

FOLLOWING OUR THIRD MISCARRIAGE IN JUNE 2017, AUSTIN and I were not ready to grow our family in any form or fashion.

The year that changed the trajectory of my life in many ways was 2018. It was the year that I took the biblical worldview class at a local church and my perspective turned fully to being a for-you-I-will *for God first* with all other for-you-I-wills branching off from Him and my desire to do all and love all *for His glory*. I simultaneously wanted to cherish 2018 for eternity, but also kick it to the curb and be left with zero memory of.

A short seven months after losing our precious baby Ruth Michelle, God began to reveal a journey that Austin and I could have never prepared ourselves for. No amount of studying or conditioning could have had us ready for this play in our lives.

We were pregnant.

I don't want to go into TMI on you. Not because I'm bashful because that's hilarious—but for the sake of those who are modest. I'll just leave it at this, yes, Austin and I know how babies are made. We know the precautions that can be taken—and we did—so when I say this was a one-in-a-million chance, it truly was.

Given our history with miscarriages and monthly fertility treatments, Austin and I are very aware of the hundreds of bodily functions that must be in perfect alignment with the stars in the sky for conception to occur.

But come on now, let's just get down to the meat of the matter—it takes a mighty God to create life. No human or shot sequence can guarantee it to happen in a month's time—but when it's God's timing, it will. He is the forever Creator and Sustainer of life.

That sentence is much easier for me to voice currently in my mommy career. Through our years of fertility struggles and loss of babies, you could find me biting my lip and my heart racing with questions of *Why not?* as I proclaimed God's sovereignty. Sister, if you're currently in this season of lip biting and a racing, questioning heart, *I see you.* I'm praying for that heart of yours. When Satan throws lies at you, remember that you are not alone and he has no dominion over you. You are a child of the one true King who wants good for you.

Austin and I were elated at this revealing of our miraculously positive pregnancy test, yet cautiously aware of what could come of the pregnancy.

I hated the way Satan tried (and usually succeeded) to rob us of joy upon the appearing of a plus sign on a pregnancy test. It's not at all how I had pictured my life going. For all my life I had seen commercials of couples smile-crying as they stared in wonder at the plus sign on the test stick. Our history led us to stand on cold bathroom tile flabbergasted and awkward in our bipolar reactions. We knew the heartache that it *could* end in, and we knew the joy that it *could* bring.

The most important thing we knew at this point was that we were 100 percent out of control. God had demonstrated that loud and clear to us through our baby Ruth's life.

Austin and I were over the moon thankful for the place that God had us in on our faith journeys at this point and time. Though our knees could still be found knocking, our hearts felt bolder and feistier than times past. We were ready to stand toe-to-toe with Satan's mind games and tell him to get the heck out of our way.

After our walk with Ruth's pregnancy, we knew that God had absolute purpose for this baby's life, just as He did for Ruth's.

Friends, our purpose isn't numbered and qualified by days of breathing on this earth.

Austin began to pull out the Rubbermaids from the attic—we needed to rewash and hang our baby girl clothes collection. Duh! Of course, we were having a *girl*. Double X chromosome for life in our household.

Once we made it past the first trimester checkups, our anxieties calmed a smidge, but we still held our emotional breath.

At our twenty-week anatomy ultrasound, Austin held my hand to his lips as the sonographer squeezed that warm gel on my growing pooch. Our palms quit sweating upon seeing that flicker of a heartbeat on the big screen, and we felt the freedom to breathe and talk, so we began chatting it up with the lady holding the magic wand of an ultrasound probe.

Come to find out she had scanned high-risk pregnancies for a decade prior to taking this position within our clinic. Boy, did we feel like we hit the jackpot that day, as she had great wisdom and experience. She was so good about enlightening us to the various shades of black and white on the screen, as well as which part was up or down.

That is, until she was hovering the probe over our baby's heart.

Not only was the once warm goopy gel starting to feel cool and unpleasant, but I immediately felt a wave of panic rush through my veins, making me feel that something was off.

I didn't like it. Not a single bit.

Austin was as supportive and encouraging as ever. He deemed the sonographer's lack of explaining at that point in the assessment, to timeliness and the need to focus on all the boxes that she had to check off before sending her report over to the radiologist.

Please.

I appreciated his words of comfort, yet deep down I didn't buy them for a second.

The following day, I left for a women's retreat where I was given the opportunity to share my story of how I saw God's love during and after our pregnancy with Ruth, despite everything that happened.

Little did I know that all my months of reading God's Word and preparing to speak about God's love to a room full of ladies was preparation and a word for my own heart. I thought I was getting to encourage women with the publicizing of our encounters with the Lord, but ultimately, God was keeping *me* in deep focus on remembering His love for me—in the good times and the bad. I had been growing deep roots of biblical perspective in my own heart.

The Monday following the weekend women's retreat, I received the phone call.

On the other end of the line, I recognized the voice of our obstetrician. Having worked in the medical field, I knew firsthand that it takes a special time and circumstance for a doctor to pick up the phone and call patients with *normal* results.

My stomach was a bag of needles—painful with each inhale.

"Mrs. White, the ultrasound revealed a possible hole in your baby's heart. We'd like to get you in with a specialist for a more detailed ultrasound to see exactly what's going on with the baby's blood flow."

That day we were put on the schedule to see a maternal-fetal specialist.

I racked my nursing brain to make sense of this puzzle, even though I was missing seven out of the ten pieces. I would google *heart conditions*—and that was dumb. Get off the Google if you're trying to diagnose yourself or a loved one. I learned that the hard way. Put down the computer mouse. It can be torturous grounds where the devil loves to meet you. Google itself is not evil, but trying to diagnose yourself with no key words to search is. Talk about trying to find a needle in a haystack.

We saw the specialist a week later and she gave us a diagnosis. It was way worse than a hole in the heart. In fact, in our scenario, a hole in her heart would have been tremendously beneficial.

Our baby girl had transposition of the great arteries.

Austin explains the diagnosis best. Being a home builder, he said it was a plumbing problem. Her main plumbing lines (the aorta and main pulmonary artery) were mixed up. Meaning, her oxygenated blood continually circulated from one side of her heart to her lungs, one side of her heart to her lungs. Which left the other side of her heart pumping all unoxygenated blood out to the remaining organs of her body—like the brain, kidneys, and so on. We don't have to be medical school graduates to understand that *all* organs need oxygenated blood for function and life.

Austin's witty metaphors are qualities that make me fall more in love with him each day. I wouldn't want to do this hard-as-heck life with anyone other than him.

Bottom line, for our baby girl to survive on this earth, we needed a miracle. That miracle could come by God's healing hands on her in the womb or by God's hands working through doctors in surgery as they performed her open-heart procedure immediately following her birth. Without major intervention, our baby was not going to live long once born.

While she was connected to me, she was perfectly fine and thriving because the umbilical cord was providing the blood flow to her and handling the blood circulation factor. But the minute the umbilical cord was cut, she would be a blue baby.

I learned very quickly that this could be another scenario that ended in heaven gaining a new angel, and our family left with no baby—just my empty uterus and arms.

I was so frustrated with God as Austin and I sat dumbfounded and eyes full of tears in the parking lot after leaving that appointment. My perspective was not good. I was in a terribly gloomy and *Why me?* kind of way.

Here we go *again*—we were so happy and content! Our family was growing in faith. Our prayer life and heart posture were thriving (or so I thought). We were finally starting to live fully with hands open and hearts abandoned for the Lord.

My thoughts of contentment should have been my first red flag, because our hearts and minds can't stretch and grow if we don't move.

Friends, life is *rough*.

All of our hearts—mine, Austin's, and the twins'—were in love with the precious gift of life that performed gymnastic routines daily within my tummy. But the revealing of a diagnosis and textbook explanations quickly turned our bright and excited state to one of darkness and trembling.

With the loss of our three babies, we'd had no idea of possible abnormalities or red flags. With this pregnancy, we were well aware of the anomalies.

A period of mourning had begun. And I hated it.

I wasn't ever known as Lauren the Lamenter, but at this point in life, I was beginning to understand what she would look like. The encourager and cheerleader spirit within me that had always pushed forward in the wins or losses of life felt strangled. Someone had snatched my pom-poms and I was ready to throw my megaphone.

Here's the best visual I can conjure up to explain my deepest feels: There I was, a cheerleader standing on the sidelines of life's game. Up until this point, I was all-teeth-showing smiling and watching the pursuit on the field, as our team/my family/society was working hard for a victory.

I'd turn to the beaming stadium lights to find a rowdy crowd of fans below. Whoopin' and hollerin' support-ers—those are my people! I love a noisy bunch. Spectators were sharing nachos and cheering with their Cokes as they watched our team drive forward for a win in life, despite the failed plays that transpired here and there.

I couldn't help but grin as I scanned my life's stadi-um. Of course, there were those goober fans/friends/

family members sprinkled throughout the bleachers who are lacking in team spirit. They'd try to throw off my perspective by keeping my focus strictly on the pessimistic parts of the game. I would shrug and brush it off because I know that they just need a handful of M&M's and the freedom to let themselves act a bit silly for them to find the merriment and appreciation of team sports and doing life together. *Kindly.*

Our team is made up of humans. Therefore, we do make mistakes during plays which can lead to upsets and setbacks. Yet overall, things are pretty square and headed in the right direction.

As I pivoted my head from the stands to turn and watch our team on the field, I saw a whopping six-foot-two 250-pound linebacker headed straight down my path. From what I could see, there's no slowing down his speed before he reached me. And the look of determination behind that face mask looked meaner than a Tasmanian devil.

Every bit of my face resembled a deer in the headlights.

The merciless, charging linebacker was our baby girl Julianna's diagnosis.

I was utterly terrified as I watched a potential disaster unfold in slow motion.

I was past the point of no return. There was no sneak play or magic chant that could stop this giant in its tracks. The play was going to have to unfold in one way or another.

Two bits, four bits, six bits, a dollar—all for a fairy tale–happy life with no hiccups or suffering, stand up and holler!

Woooooo-hoooooo!

A sea of participants spring to their feet clapping in agreement, like a line of seals at Sea World, demanding attention and oneness. Piercing whistles, unruly air horns, and cowbells can be heard miles down the main drag from the stadium, as the leaders of the cheer section incite the crowd.

If you were one of those fans who willfully stood in accord with most of the stadium ticket holders, I gotta break it to you, that two bits cheer for this life that we live is going to have to be reworked.

We can't cheer and lead one another with words that are unattainable and silly.

This "life game" that I'm referring to is what you and I do every day. It's the mundane business of clocking in and out at work and trimming back shrubs in the flower beds.

It's the gathering at birthday parties and a golf score card showing an avian theme, as you scored under par. These fun-filled days drive us to jump in the air with celebration and delight.

Yet we mustn't forget that life will herd us to encounters of defeat and struggle, demanding us to take a knee during the game. Sometimes, we're caught in a breath hold as we watch paramedics enter the scene.

If we're going to remain in this game of life and have a levelheaded, realistic mindset going into each play, it's going to take some cheers and funny chants for us to manage to walk out of this game with our heads held high. We must also anticipate the blindsided hits of circumstances.

Most importantly, we need to address our character in the game. Good sportsmanship is a must.

For starters, we must have respect, be willing to learn, honor others, and practice self-control. A positive attitude is a necessity but challenging to enforce throughout the entirety of the game. Our whole team—that's you, me, and every other human in this world—must sharpen our resilience, perseverance, kindness, and inclusion in our daily grind.

Good sportsmanship isn't simply gained in the gym. There are no repetitive training activities that we can conquer prior to stepping onto the turf of life's unknowns. It's going to take some serious mental and physical focus, both on and off the field. There will be some brow-sweating and tears of apprehension and achievement.

Life's list of plays will require us to roll with the punches—and I do mean flatten-us-out literal punches.

I tell you with every joyful cell in my body, there once was a time in my life that I, too, blew an obnoxious airhorn in support of a "feel good, hurt free" philosophy for daily living. I was the cheerleader who woke up with sore cheeks and a weak voice on Saturday mornings, as I had spent the night before shouting my excitement.

However, as the chief bubble-buster in this scenario, I know that my sad truths can surface all your feels. It's not meanness that drives me to bring you these wayward emotions. It's quite the opposite rather.

I come to you with a healed heart overflowing with hard-learned love. I'm determined to keep a stable perspective in this wayward game of life, and I will remain your constant cheerleader as our life training skills unfold on these pages. After all, cheerleaders stick by the sides of their team and community at all times. Not just in the victorious ones.

We're in this together! For every cheer and chapter that contains hard truth, there will be a verse to follow with hope and togetherness.

If you've ever found yourself in the path of destruction and looking straight into the face of danger, you're not alone. But let me tell you something happy. Even when we're caught in moments where we don't know what the outcome will be, God, the Head Coach of this game, holds the playbook of all playbooks. Now, that doesn't mean that He's going to bend down and show us the final score of the game before it's over.

Remember that whole character-building thing? It's moments of struggle where growing and stretching pains begin. Those muscles start to tremor and burn—there is damage and injury. Yet it's in those breaking down times that our body yields greater muscle mass and size.

I can assure you I was sweating bullets and 100 percent overwhelmed during the play of life where we learned of Julianna's heart defect. There was a lot of muscle ripping going on—mainly of those in my emotional heart.

Was our baby going to receive a miracle and be able to live a semi-normal life? What if the surgery she needed was unsuccessful? Would she need a heart transplant?

There were days I couldn't comprehend my reality because there were too many unknowns. Yet in that moment of unprecedented terror, I knew I had my fellow cheerleaders by my side. The fans populating the bleachers were on my team as well (except for the goober ones, of course).

Friend, I pray that you, too, recognize the teammates and community that surround you. Those like-minded individuals are going to be the ones you can talk daily life with on the good days, and they'll be the first to your side on the days you get knocked to the ground and can't move.

More than anything, I pray that you can find rest in the fact that God always holds the ultimate playbook in His possession. There are no worldly trick plays or tactics against you that the Enemy can pull and surprise God with.

The illnesses.

The affairs.

The destroying and dividing of families.

The depression.

The substance abuse.

The mockery from the mouths of "friends."

The suicidal thoughts.

The self-loathing.

They're all plays in the Enemy's hands.

To us, the future is unknown. To God, our futures are part of history, because He already knows the outcome of our life. Life's playbook is under His control.

Because of God's perpetual love for us, we don't have to be consumed with the time clock, touchbacks, or holdings on the field. We just need to keep our eyes and ears tuned in to our Head Coach.

Check It

1: When is a time in life that you can remember a giant linebacker headed in your direction at full speed? Maybe it was a pending medical diagnosis or anxiously awaiting a job evaluation. Whatever it was, can you see God's grace covering you in the shaking unknowns?

2: What verse do you find yourself going to in the Bible when you're walking a trapeze across a fiery unknown below you? Share that verse with a friend today.

Affirmation (Come on, sister! Say it loud! Say it proud!)

God, you are with me here.

God, you were with me there.

God, you are with me everywhere in my life.

Through the happy and the hurt, *you are with me,*
and you love me without end.

I'm claiming and acting on these words in Psalm 77:11–14 (ESV), "I will remember the deeds of the Lord; yes, I will remember your wonders of old. I will ponder all your work, and meditate on your mighty deeds. Your way, O God, is holy. What god is great like our God? You are the God who works wonders . . ."

Say What?

MY WEDNESDAY PODCAST WAS TURNED UP LOUD AS I jogged in place. I was feeling hyped about the topic of essentialism.

"You know you're not going anywhere, right?" Austin had just walked in.

Au contraire. According to my trusty Apple Watch, I'd taken 1,400 steps, so far . . . 1,400 steps to nowhere.

So, yeah, he was correct. My jogging in place was getting me nowhere, but I completely accepted that fact. I grinned and continued my jog in the corner of our peacock blue–painted bedroom.

When I was running on the soccer field in my elementary days, my daddy told me I ran like a girl. There's a heaping dose of truth in that statement, yet the way he mimicked me looked like a prissy *Tyrannosaurus rex* galivanting through a field. That view has disturbed me ever since. I will allow no gawking at my prissy, *T-Rex* self. Therefore, from that moment on, I decided to decline any engagement that would require me to run in front of other people.

However, I'm 100 percent confident with my jogging in a private place routine.

To state the obvious, I'm not an Ironman, but I read about someone who is.

Twenty-one-year-old Chris Nikic landed himself a title in the Guinness World Records after completing the Florida Ironman triathlon. Finishing off a total distance of 140.6 miles, Chris bravely pressed through a 2.4-mile swim, a 112-mile bike ride, and a 26.2-mile run in 16 hours 46 minutes and 9 seconds—a mere 14 minutes faster than the cutoff for qualification.[15]

Chris reached his personal goal of finishing under the 17-hour mark *and* he earned himself a spot in the Guinness World Records! Absolutely remarkable!

Personally, I feel really accomplished when my Apple Watch commends me for the few miles a day that I walk. Pretty sure my watch would straight up explode if I completed an Ironman, because it has never had to calculate that much exercise.

Finishing an Ironman is a massive achievement, but even more astonishing is the fact that Chris Nikic was the first person with Down syndrome to do so. As a result of his Down syndrome, Chris had an open-heart surgery at just under five months old. He had four major ear surgeries due to narrow ear canals. And Chris had to go through many therapy sessions just to learn how to hold a fork. All his life, Chris has had to work extremely hard to overcome instances that were not stacked in his favor.

That brave and resilient man is a gifted Ironman today.

Talk about a powerhouse of an overcomer! I wish I had been present to wave posters and holler for him during his monstrous achievement.

Way to go, Chris!

Even though I'm not bound to find my name in the Guinness World Records for an incredible feat, I do compete in my own sorts of challenges. In fact, we all endure various Ironman triathlons in life.

Maybe it's completing a triathlon to good health.

Perhaps conquering the career world is your feat.

Or what about the plain ol' long distance of everyday highs and lows like handling the issue of a car that requires new brakes today and a bank account that won't see a deposit for another ten days?

For some, the family gatherings have become so stressful and tense over the years, we'd rather attempt to run four miles through a desert with a ten-pound weighted vest on than sit at that awkward family table for one more event.

As humans, we all venture in athletic contests to some degree.

A lot of conditioned muscles are needed to cross the finish line of a triathlon. Turns out, most of our individual triathlons in life, are driven mainly by one muscle.

The heart.

We have a triathlete living at our house. Don't be fooled by her hazel eyes and puppy-ear ponytails. Our daughter

Julianna completed her first Ironman triathlon of life when she was less than two months old. She's our heart warrior babe.

Baby girl came into this world on her own timing. Who needs a due date from a medical professional when you have headstrong children who officiate their own debut?

Two days prior to a scheduled cesarean section, my resting heart rate was staying beyond the safety bounds in the pregnancy game, so that September day we went in for Julianna to be born.

Come to find out, she had some issues of her own brewing, so really and truly, my heightened heart rate and discomfort were a blessing in disguise. The doctors and nurses knew the extra setbacks she was already bringing to the scene with a "hazardous and red flagged" congenital heart defect diagnosis. While in utero, Julianna had swallowed meconium and her heart was in an abnormal rhythm. As soon as she was born, the medical staff had a lot of stabilizing to do before she could even be transferred to Arkansas Children's Hospital to begin that stretch of her race.

There's someone way bigger than me in charge of timing for life events. Praise God for His control of the clock and calendar and my lack of it!

Once stabilized from delivery, our girl took an ambulance chariot ride to the children's hospital down the road. Sister girl was bougie right out of the chute and we adore every ounce of her high expectation self.

For seven days, Austin and I sat bedside to Julianna in the cardiovascular intensive care unit. We watched her delicate hand wrapped around our index fingers. Occasionally we would kiss the top of her hair, but we didn't want to overstimulate and stress her body. It was a fine line of physical affection and what was best for our little love.

When she was eight days old, we held Julianna in our arms for the very first time. Man, what a realization I had of how many cuddles and skin-to-skin care sessions I had taken for granted with our twins immediately following their birth.

Can't we all get that way? Once something or someone is physically out of reach or off-limits to us, we realize all the blessings and good stuff we had going for us all along.

It's our human nature.

It's our perspective in the moment.

Thank goodness we have mentors, friends, coaches, and loved ones who help keep us in check and aware in our day-to-day happenings.

We all have our people who offer us perspective in life. Let's be mindful that we surround ourselves with the ones who will give us the healthy doses of blood-boiling truths—and also eye-opening grace.

As we rallied and prayed for our Julianna throughout her triathlon, our family was being loved on hourly.

It wasn't the happiest of places to be with my hormonal self and Austin's stressed-out mind, but church friends, family members, and strangers came to our side in the waiting room of that CVICU floor. They made themselves available to us, even though they knew it could be like walking into a land mine of hurt and awkwardness. We had enough food and gift cards to feed the US president and his cabinet. Daily. Our family is crazy blessed and thankful for our village.

Let's challenge ourselves every day to begin new triathlons of neighboring and befriending.

To go outside and make a new friend is way more fun than cleaning that sticky goop and those saltine cracker crumbs from our refrigerator drawers. Those crumbs will be homey and happy right where they are. As humans, if we're not connected and engaged with wholesome, uplifting beings in our daily walk, we will wander. It's in that aimless moving about where the lies of Satan creep in and start to internally beat us down.

Leave the messes. Run to people.

We're going to be the generation to intentionally entangle our surrounding mankind with endless applause and words of mercy. Oh, and we're going to raise the next generations to follow in that plot—so, there. Get back, Satan.

Though shocking and scary to Austin and me at times, our doctors and medical staff never skipped a beat or acted too surprised by the offbeats of this medical song we were living out with our littlest love's heart defect.

Austin and I were beading sweat and in the throes of our own Ironman.

On day two of Julianna's life, she almost died from a collapsed lung.

That day, Julianna earned herself a "troublemaker" flag in her medical chart. The staff took her collapsing lung llama-drama event as attention seeking. Halfway kidding, but not really. They called it correctly. But, again, we sure are thankful for her strong, spitfire self.

Julianna had her first lifesaving cath lab procedure performed at two hours old, but her next huge goal was to have the open-heart procedure.

Obviously, a sick, collapsed lung is not a good candidate for being put on the heart-lung bypass machine, so essentially she had to start back with basic training and healing before getting on the surgery schedule.

After twenty-two days of resting and strength training, Julianna's surgery fired off an intense plunge into her Ironman.

On surgery day, families walk bedside with their child as the OR team wheels them to the end of the ICU hallway. It is there that the final hugs and kisses are given, and many tears are shed from little and big people alike. The oversized brown doors swing wide to reveal a line of blue tile below, as if to say "Stop! No passing of parents beyond this point!" As the parent of the contestant running that race to the operating room, you're never prepared for your turn at the end of the hall. Once that oversized bed on wheels rounds the corner, you try to take a million mental photos of your loved one. Even if the worst of the worst doesn't play out, you have no idea how long your child will be sedated and medicated, masking the person you know they are within.

Julianna's six hour–long stretch in the operating room went as smoothly as possible. Obviously not by her own training or prepping, but by the hand of a gracious God and the wisdom, compassion, and skill set of individuals used as God's instruments in that OR.

Her next leg of the race took place post-operatively in the intensive care unit. We were prepared for all kinds of "normal recovery setbacks," from heart rate irregularities, to blood clots, and post-operative infections.

I'll never forget the first time I saw her after the surgery.

The number of IV pumps beside her eight-pound body seemed greater than the add-in options at your local Starbucks coffee joint. Even as a nurse who felt at home amongst the flashing lights and beeping machines, it was completely overwhelming to see part of my soul lying there so painfully fragile.

Austin and I literally watched the *lub-dub, lub-dub* pumping of J's walnut-sized heart. Her chest was not yet closed; only a protective dressing overlay the opening. This is done as a precaution, in case too many normal setbacks lead a patient to need another trip into the operating room.

"Mommy, I think I got a paper cut putting together my craft!" demands the preschooler across the island.

"Sister, let me see." My lips purse and my eyes do a 360-degree roll as I assess the dry paper cut that is one-eighteenth of an inch deep. "Girl, please. You're fine. Grab that glue stick and keep on building that snowman."

It goes without saying, I'm working to rebuild my sympathy muscles for any injuries that do not reveal a dangling appendage or visible organ.

Zero. Zilch. That's the number of glitches Julianna encountered postoperatively. An absolute miracle from God.

Now, don't hear me say that this was a smooth sailing kind of adventure because it was far from that. It took what seemed like weeks to wean J off her medications. After all, since her first breath on earth, she was medicated. Watching the withdrawal symptoms come from her eight-pound body can't mentally be erased.

As Austin was headed back to the CVICU from the hospital's cafeteria one afternoon, he and his fellow elevator passengers were chatting in an attempt to keep the awkward silence low. It started with the casual, "How are you today?" and "That Styrofoam box you're holding sure smells tasty." Before reaching the fourth floor, the conversation ended with a man confiding to the elevator bunch that he was headed back to his child's room, where they would be turning off the life support.

Austin walked back into Julianna's hospital room and looked like he had just been sucker punched. His face was drained of color. After hearing the details of his elevator encounter, our helicopter parenting strings were tightened and our internal conversations with God escalated in volume of both material and sound.

Having a child in that intensive care unit forever changed us. It changed the intensity of how we love our children and how we love the families who also sit in those CVICU chairs not knowing what "event" will happen next in their loved one's body.

During our hospital stay, I felt I was losing my mind—but now, I can sit back and acknowledge the strength and character chiseling that was taking place.

Perspective needs time to sizzle out and cool down.

Give yourself grace in your perspective's cooking process.

As Austin and I sat in amazement of our baby girl's unusually smooth progress following open-heart surgery, we watched families scream and bawl in the waiting room as their loved ones passed away. These are moments in time that we wish we could unsee and unhear, but we're working to use those scars as fuel and compassion to serve families with sick kiddos. Heck, we're using those nightmares as fuel to better serve and love on people who suffer from any fragile situation in life.

You better believe I was all kinds of scrappy and questioning at the feet of God through this process. One minute I'd have an overwhelming sense of peace in the unknown ticking of the minute hand. The next minute I could feel pressure building in my chest and my heart would race. And I literally couldn't think straight, as it felt like such a fog. At times I looked like a wig-wearing Frankenstein walking the hospital halls.

Outside Julianna's hospital window, we could see a main interstate that meandered through our capital city. Every day, cars were bustling down the lanes. People were headed to clock in to their nine-to-five jobs, while others were headed for playdates at the park. Meanwhile, inside the hospital walls, our family and countless others felt as if our lives were on complete hold. It's as if time stood still but also moved at a brisk speed as emergencies unfolded at the drop of a hat.

Can't we all feel frozen in times of trial and hurt, even though the rest of the world is coasting down life's road with what seems like not a single care?

There are going to be times of running our triathlon where we get passed by the lady in the yellow tank top and Lululemon leggings who appears completely put together from head to toe. Though we're all running the same race path but under different training statuses, we may feel one deep breath away from hurling while others are breezing by us.

Remember, we're not alone on our journey.

Let's focus on finishing strong in our lane. All while cheering for others who are pushing forward in their lanes to complete their race.

Here's a part of Chris Nikic's Florida triathlon story that gave me goosebumps.

Ten miles into the running portion of the Florida Ironman, Chris stopped and felt as if he couldn't continue. His body hurt and he wanted to take off the tether to his pacer/trainer who was competing alongside him. Chris's coach knew he was going to need a bigger dose of encouragement than he could provide.

Chris's dad was brought onto the scene. Immediately, his dad embraced him with arms wide open and the strength of love that only a father can provide. His dad had dropped whatever conversation or thought process he was zoned in on, and he ran. He ran to his son with arms wide open.

In that moment, Chris's dad portrayed the idea that we must leave the messes and run to the people.

Let's leave our comfort and run to the people.

As Chris fought back tears of pain and possible defeat, his dad simply said, "Let's keep walking. How's my boy?" With his arm around Chris, they slowly walked toward the finish line. While runners passed on the left and right, this father/son duo kept their focus on the goal and their words full of truth and grace.

Chris's dad affirmed him in the fact that his pains were real, but another reality on that day was his being titled an Ironman. He spoke words to his son that assured him of his readiness and the overflowing amount of support that stood for him along the race path.

The affirmation of Chris's abilities and words of empowerment that his dad lavished on him lit a fire within Chris. He crossed the finish line within the allotted race time and became an official Ironman on that November day. It wasn't about the title, it was about the accomplishing of a goal of normalcy and inclusion, for someone who can so quickly be excluded and marked as not fully equipped.

This story is such a testament to hard work, determination, and encouragement.

In our grueling courses with our baby Julianna, our family was being cheered for and supported throughout the race. We had the boldest and most dedicated prayer warriors praying with and for us.

On days when Austin and I just didn't know how much more we could bear, a nurse, respiratory therapist, or even the unit supervisor would come alongside us and speak words of hope into our souls.

So I'll ask you. What stretch of life's triathlon are you on? Do you have someone swimming beside you as you take on the currents of the water below? Is there a friend to help you switch out a bike tire when you go from riding a bicycle to a unicycle? Sure, these are all hypotheticals, but bottom line, we all need a support system along our racecourse.

Want to hear some God-writing that gives me chill bumps? One of Julianna's heart surgeons and his family are now some of our closest friends that we get to do life with. Her surgeon's wife is one of my dearest friends and confidants. Together they have four fun-filled kiddos. Their oldest daughter is in high school and treats our kiddos like siblings of her own. Another daughter is a year younger than our twins and they laugh and play whenever they're together. Their son is a trooper of a little man, as he is totally outnumbered by girls when our families get together. But our active crews have no problem playing together as they enjoy games and running circles around us adults. Their youngest daughter and Julianna are attached at the hip when running on the playground at school or doing twirls on the dance studio floor. It's the most beautiful and heartwarming thing for me to see how God so kindly provided us with such a brilliant and skilled doctor during Julianna's heart surgery—but His kindness didn't stop there. He went on to allow us deep relationship with the doctor and his entire family.

Tears. OK. Reel it in, Lauren.

If we all take to heart our responsibility to show love and respect everyone around us, we will have way more contestants successfully completing their races.

Most importantly, when we find ourselves hunched over with our hands on our knees, gasping for breath, tears streaming down our face, and feeling the desire to scream from the excruciating pain within, we must remember that our heavenly Father is *there*.

Just as Chris's dad jumped onto the course, our God is there to wrap us up in His arms of security and love when we call out to Him. Close your eyes and visualize God holding your face in His hands and saying, "How's my kiddo?" And He stays right beside us as we walk forward in life. He does it, y'all.

The question is this: are we viewing life through the right lens that reveals and acknowledges God's presence? There will be loads of opportunities for us to come beside someone who is hurting and wrestling with the struggles of this world. Though it's been a hard lesson for me to learn, we're not always supposed to stand there and *rah rah!* them in hopes of boosting their esteem. We're there to say, "How are you?"

There are stretches in life that we have to push through the discomfort of the bad days before we get back to the good days. Let's help make sure that people know they're seen in all stretches of their life's triathalon.

The Bible tells us to call upon the Lord—to be still and silent. The maker of the waters that Chris Nikic plunged and the landscape that he navigated during his Ironman is the same Creator we can call out to for comfort and strength and who will fight for us in our time of need.

God redirects us to our goals.

He assures us of who we are *in Him.*

And He whoops, hollers, and wholeheartedly encourages us alongside every triathlon we face in life.

Check It

1: What triathlon are you pushing through today?

2: Is there a particular stretch of a life triathlon/ hardship when you remember a moment of God's presence being unmistakable? Chris's dad said, "How's my boy?" What did God speak to you?

Affirmation (Come on, sister! Say it loud! Say it proud!)

God, you are with me here.

God, you were with me there.

God, you are with me everywhere in my life.

Through the happy and the hurt, *you are with me,* and you love me without end.

I'm claiming and acting on these words in Psalm 77:11–14 (ESV), "I will remember the deeds of the Lord; yes, I will remember your wonders of old. I will ponder all your work, and meditate on your mighty deeds. Your way, O God, is holy. What god is great like our God? You are the God who works wonders . . ."

Bring in the Medics

"*ARE YOU SURE YOU DON'T WANT ANY BREAKFAST?*" I asked Austin. "I can pour a fancy bowl of cereal or scramble some eggs."

Austin again denied the need for sustenance and made his rounds of kissing all his girlies before scurrying off to the demands of work world.

For two days, Austin had been fasting. He couldn't explain exactly why he felt led to do so, but he was certain that God wanted him more focused on Him than a short stack of pancakes. Because he is a huge breakfast lover, Austin's turning down the first meal of the day was spraining my brain.

Seventeen years into loving this man, he continues to inspire me with his discipline and oneness with the Holy Spirit. Y'all, on this day of Austin's breakfast refusal, I was about to get a lesson in how the Lord speaks.

For years I felt as if the squeaking of crickets and croaking of frogs outside our house was way more prevalent than the voice of God. Turns out, it was my own heart and ears that weren't primed and functioning correctly. God was actually so close and present to me, He didn't even have to speak in the normal conversation volume of sixty decibels. He was so near a whisper was all He required.

A loud and long forty-five-minute stretch after Austin's exit from our home, the twins and I were headed to the grocery store for our click-list pickup order. Whoop! Whoop! Talk about a gift to mankind, to be able to click Goldfish, Dole bananas, and bag salad from an app, all to pick them up from the comfort of your car. America, we are winning.

While en route from rural Arkansas to the nearest urban grocery store, I talked with my momma and daddy on the phone. Y'all already know how much my momma and I talked. The same was true with my daddy, too. In my working outside the home days, I had a bonus conversation with Daddy every morning and afternoon. It has *never* been unusual for me to talk with them three plus times a day on the phone—from my college days all the way to my married and parenting days. Our communication and relationships were constant and close.

After hearing of their morning happenings with their twin fur baby Labradors, we continued with business as usual. Part of the conversation showcased their customary, irrational giving fashion. They said that Austin and I could have one of the cribs from their house for our Julianna, who was set to be born in three short months.

Knowing Julianna's heart defect and all the risks to come, I had been postponing most nesting tasks that expectant mothers are typically giddy over and throwing themselves into. I'm ashamed to admit this but I was scared to allow myself to get too excited. The last thing I wanted to do was decorate a precious nursery for our princess, only to come home to pink walls, satin ribbons, and no baby to enjoy it all. My heart was so timid and my perspective so skewed.

Some days, outings with the sisters are more short and sweet than others. On that day, it was straight to the store and straight home. We unloaded our bags of goods, as our treeing Walker coonhound sniffed our tracks in and out of the house.

It took me a while to grasp this but allowing our kiddos to help with everyday tasks is indeed a good thing. It's not child abuse to have them carry in a sack of green grapes that we will eventually be dicing for their eating pleasure. Chores, if you will, can actually instill teamwork, responsibility, and life skills. Who would've known? Sure, don't hand them the eggs, unless your goal is to test your cleaning skills and odds of beating salmonella, but snacks and fruit will be just fine for their little limbs to tote.

We all grow by putting in the work. Even the kiddos.

And it's one hundred percent OK if we happen to laugh, sing, and have fun while we're in the grind.

In the wake of morning play and grocery sorting with the sisters, this momma needed to catch up on some breathing.

I sat my six-month preggers self down on our living room floor against the red leather ottoman. The coolness of the leather was quite refreshing on that summer day. If the sweltering heat and humidity of Arkansas summers aren't enough of a thermal challenge, multiply it by a thousand once you factor in the body heat of an additional human being growing in your uterus.

Upon the completion of returning some text messages and scheduling a much-needed haircut, it hit me. *I should be a compliant patient and go eat some ice cream.* Our maternal-fetal specialist (whom we love to pieces!) had given me strict instructions to eat all the ice cream, avocados, and cheeseburgers that I desired because if I took in fat, then our baby Julianna would get that same fat. We wanted to send in the biggest baby possible for heart surgery.

As I stood over the kitchen island, I shoveled the most splendid Blue Bell ice cream into my mouth. It consisted of the perfect ratio of dark chocolate chunks and creamy chocolatey goodness in each spoonful—so good it'll make your tongue slap your brains out. (That's a fancy phrase we use down here in the South. We prefer to keep words simple, to make things relatable and allow for everyone to feel welcome. *Wink. Wink.*)

Rays of sunshine burst through the two-months-too-dusty wooden blinds, illuminating me and my tub of fat-filled ice cream. I didn't think the day could have been any more radiant. It was a moment of calm and happy that I was soaking up in its entirety as our twin threenagers napped like angels two walls over.

My ears instantly perked up as I heard the garage door opening from the wall behind me. It had to be

Austin. But what in the world was he doing home in the middle of the day, when I knew that this day's schedule demanded his presence in three different counties?

How strange that he didn't call to let me know he was going to stop by.

In a flash, I panicked because I didn't know if I should be ashamed of my sugary indulgence, or if Austin would be proud of my "selfless" decision to fatten up our baby per the doctor's orders. To shove the evidence of ice cream and my used spoon back into the freezer or not was the most stressful moment of my day. So I thought.

I heard the door close and footsteps quickly approaching as I was in mid bite. I knew that pace of stepping as an alert to something exciting or really bad.

As I turned to look at him while trying to avoid a brain freeze from inhaling my frozen treat, I could immediately sense that something was wrong.

Very wrong.

Austin made a beeline for me and grabbed my hands. The deep stare of his eyes into mine told me that he was broken and in shock over something. The folding-in of his lips was a flashing warning sign of distress in a man normally strong and calm.

My heart raced. My stomach twisted into knots in seconds.

With my hands in his, Austin walked backwards into our living room and kept saying, "Honey, I love you so much. I need you to sit down." It felt like he said that phrase twenty times in less than fifteen seconds.

At this point, I was in full-blown panic.

I sat down on the edge of our recliner, continuously questioning, "What is it? Tell me what's wrong!"

Austin looked me in the eyes, regained his calm strength, and the words began to flow. "Honey, I just got off the phone with your mom. She's driving behind an ambulance that is taking your dad to the hospital."

My heart rate went from 105 beats per minute to 125 in three seconds.

Austin continued on. "They think he had a heart attack."

Immediately, I fell to my knees and can only remember my repetitive shrieks of, "No! No! No! No!"

A tormenting silence lagged as I began to simultaneously hold my breath and cry.

Through his own tears, Austin delivered a final bit of information. "Honey, your mom doesn't think he's going to make it."

So we sat on the living room floor and bawled. The setting that had been so bright and therapeutic a mere five minutes earlier was now a room of doom and despair.

I thought, *There's no way this is really happening. God, are you serious, right now? A baby girl is growing inside of me and she may or may not live once she's born. And now, you're going to take away my very first love? You can't take my daddy away from me—I need him—I have to have him for many more years to come. My children need their Pappy to teach them and watch them grow up! Please, God. Don't take my daddy.*

I squeezed and held on to Austin with every ounce of energy I had, while at the same time setting my body on a numbing mode. I knew that my anxiety would trigger effects in my body—such as high blood pressure and stress—that could cause my already high-risk pregnancy to rise to a whole different level of risk. The only thing I could think to do was *not feel*, so my body would not respond and cause Julianna to be born prematurely.

We prayed. It was the only thing we knew to do.

I begged and pleaded for God to save my daddy.

Dial back to that visual I shared with you of me as a cheerleader in life. More specifically, as the cheerleader who had turned to watch the game and found myself with a towering linebacker headed straight toward me.

That linebacker coming at me in slow motion represented the diagnosis of our Julianna's heart defect. Now the linebacker charging toward me was bigger and coming at an increased speed as this horrifying news of my daddy's heart attack was revealed to me.

Bam!

On the day Austin came home to tell me of my daddy's heart attack, that linebacker knocked me out cold.

On my knees in our living room floor, my cheerleader visual continued to play out. As the birds and stars began to settle from the collision of my news and the linebacker, I could see the medics and coaches standing over me like a swarm of seagulls leaning in for final dibs on those Cheez-It remains left behind by a group of beachfront spring-breakers.

Faces and lighting slowly began to come into focus, but I couldn't hear a word from the mouths of those standing above me. The two sounds that I could make out were a high pitch, ringing in my head, blended with my self-conscious saying, "What's happening? I can't breathe. Someone help! I can't breathe!"

Aside from breathlessness, I couldn't feel a single sensation, although I could see hands touching my face and raising my arms as they began to monitor my vital signs.

My entire body was numb. Metaphorically speaking. But also in a self-induced reality kind of way.

My prayers were not answered on that Tuesday afternoon when Austin came home with life-changing news. On this day I received the most unwanted yet profound lesson on the will of God.

Daddy didn't make it. The most giving, gentle, and goofball of a man that I had ever known was gone.

One year to the date of having my D&C with our baby Ruth, we buried my precious daddy.

I haven't been the same Lauren since.

I want to numb out right this minute, as all the feels of anger, hurt, confusion, and dismay surface within me. Yet after much healing grace and rewiring of my neuropathways over the last few years, I can intentionally stop and reverse my desire to numb out and not feel when I'm overcome with the reality of Daddy being gone.

Unfortunately, for years I kept my body and emotions at a standstill. I refused to allow myself to feel and truly absorb the loss and truth of my wounded life. After all, I needed to be strong for my momma, sister, and daughters.

But that's exactly what the Enemy wants us to do. He smiles and creepily shrieks in joy at the thought of my being so paralyzed and stuck in my grief that I'm limited in my range of loving others and sharing the good news of the gospel—especially when good wasn't even on my life's radar.

Time doesn't take away or heal *all* loss. Time does allow us to replay life and switch our perspective as we can step out from our hurt with scars forming and anxieties under a treatment plan.

Well, get the heck out of town, Satan! My parents raised me to be a woman of strength, great conviction, and irrationally giving of my resources.

My wounds are scarring over and my heart is being restored from its shattering, by God's unfathomable grace.

Do I have days that lead my children to walk into a room and ask me if I'm crying because I miss Pappy and Yaya? You better believe it. *Lots* and *lots* of days. And those surprise surfacing of emotions will continue for the remainder of my life.

But I'm not alone in those moments because my daughters are there and know what to do.

I see the concept of the faith of a child lived out in their day-to-day happenings. Our girlies stretch me in every direction possible—from patience and grace giving to my own reality of God's goodness and existence.

Those darling babes take my moments of weakness and despair, and they empower me with their love and strength that come from their pure hearts. They believe God to always be good and right, just like they learn from the Bible. They run and bring me a picture of my momma and daddy or the security stuffed animal (a polar bear) that I have on loan to them from my childhood. Their little hearts tell them to provide genuine comfort and encouragement when they see me ugly crying and trying to catch a breath as I long for one more phone call or dinner with my parents.

Y'all, they're so young. Yet in their hearts is so. much. *good!*

That pure goodness and concern for the well-being of others cannot be taught. It's embedded in the makeup of us all, from the God that forged us from head to toe. What we do have to teach ourselves is to not let the negative voices of the world override our instinct and call to act in love and virtue.

Do you, too, find yourself in amazement of the joy and perseverance of children around you? Maybe it's a neighbor—a child running through the aisles at church or Walmart—or your own family member who triggers your mind and heart to stop and ponder on the brokenness in this life from a different perspective.

In the smack-dab middle of Daddy's passing and all that followed with Julianna's birth, I was numbing out from not only the hard things in life, but the good things as well.

In my numbed-out mind and spirit, I missed the warm and exciting days of the girls receiving their first puppy for Christmas. In my self-induced numbness, I missed soaking up their genuine magic-filled eyes as they romped around with a ten-pound fur ball. And I've always been a squealer when I see pets—because the passion in my heart for them cannot be contained, so it explodes through my vocal cords. I was not in a good state. But, boy, am I thankful for pictures that help me relive in those joyful moments now that my numbness is lifted and my perspective is more in focus.

Let me help connect dots.

Sometimes you can't see the forest for the trees, yes?

At times it's difficult to pick out beauty in the struggles of life.

It's like looking at the inside of a patterned sock. The inside of the sock looks like a mess of multicolored threads crisscrossing throughout. Yet when you flip it right side out, the beauty of a well-defined and thought-out pattern is revealed.

Our lives are comparable to socks. Let's just refer to them as life socks. That's a funsy kind of word and we all need funsy-ness in our lives.

Right now, living life in this broken world, we tend to see the inward messiness of our socks. But someday, our life sock will be flipped right side out to expose an intertwining of purpose and appeal.

As you're suffering through your own personal trials, keep thinking about that life sock.

Your life will not always be so heavy burdened and frayed.

Keep surrounding yourself with people who lift you up along your trek of hurt and struggle. Those people are the very people whom God very intentionally intertwines into your life sock, and later unveils their specific purpose and artistry in your world.

Raise your hand if you've ever had the wind knocked out of you.

Surely, we all have at one point or another.

For some of us, we misjudged the distance from one monkey bar to the next and found ourselves breathless and flat on our back.

Other times, we're given some shocking or tragic news that literally takes our breath away from the intensity of our emotions played out.

Fun fact—did you know that when you get the breath knocked out of you, it's not your lungs causing the holdup, it's actually your diaphragm. When we experience some form of blunt force to the abdomen, pressure is put on a group of nerves known as the solar plexus, which in turn causes the diaphragm to spasm. A whacked-out diaphragm = difficulty with the inhaling and exhaling process.

In essence, we still have life and breath in our lungs when the wind is knocked out of us.

In life, we're going to get the wind knocked out of us. We will experience numerous, breathless moments. Our air exchanging will come to a standstill.

That June afternoon standing over a tub of ice cream when Austin came home early to tell me about my daddy, I absolutely had the wind knocked out of me. Austin and several friends and family members had to verbally remind me to breathe in those initial days.

Yet the God who spoke our very lives into existence with His own breath is the same God who is sustaining us in our gasping moments of life. Though we have a sensation of breathlessness, *there is still life within us.*

Our sustaining God is who stirred within Austin and gave him the instruction to fast for two days prior to my Daddy's passing, in preparation of having him so closely fixated on God and His sovereignty, for the tragedy to come. God was eight steps ahead of the game—He knew Austin's need to step up and lead on a whole new level following Daddy's passing. I'm so thankful for Austin's perspective to surrender and be obedient to God's leading in his life.

He's the God who knows the number of days to each of our lives.

When the hurts of this world take us down, we need strength to take another breath or step. When we go numb from the intense amount of pain, we need to remember that scripture from Nehemiah 8: "... the joy of the LORD is your strength" (v. 10, CSB). Remember, what that tells us is how joyful our God is. And He's joyful because of His creation of and love for *us*. Therefore, when life punches us so hard we don't know how to physically get out of bed, we *can* swing our feet out and set them on the floor to start the moving forward process. Not because of anything on our own. But because the joy that God finds in us serves as the outlet for our strength.

When we wonder how we could possibly live another day as circumstances around us have changed so drastically—through the loss of a loved one, the loss of a job, the diagnosis of cancer, or the ordeal of a bankruptcy—remember that your God sees you.

The One who paints daily sunrises is also mesmerized and thrilled at your very breath and being in this moment. He can always provide you with the strength to carry on.

One of my mentors that I have had the honor to watch live life for over a decade now has endured some *rough* times. She lost a baby, her husband passed away when her three children were young, and that was after her first marriage, which was physically abusive. Years later, she herself was diagnosed with cancer, and the removal of that tumor left her with some facial nerve damage.

If you saw the energy, the radiance, the joy, and the servanthood of this woman today, you would tell me that I was a crazy person for giving you those above snippets of her life hurts and challenges. She is such a beautiful, bold, bighearted follower of Jesus. Her life sock is slowly being flipped right side out to reveal the purpose and wonder of her tangled threads and she mindfully wears a biblical perspective to be able to fully see the beauty from those mixed-up threadings.

Not one of us can see the entirety of our life sock, yet. But one day . . . one day, the intricate and ravishing design of the inward threads will be revealed to us.

Yes, our losses and adversities are displayed now.

And they stink.

But we can stick this out together. Not by our own capabilities, but by the strength given to us from the God who has an insane amount of joy in you and me.

Check It

1: What threading of events and people do you see today in your life's sock?

2: Do you have a friend or loved one who recently went through a life storm? Maybe you can think of someone who is in the middle of a deep storm? Pick up the phone or a pen and paper and reach out to them to let them know how loved and seen they are. Remind them that they are not alone.

Affirmation (Come on, sister! Say it loud! Say it proud!)

God, you are with me here.

God, you were with me there.

God, you are with me everywhere in my life.

Through the happy and the hurt, *you are with me,*
and you love me without end.

I'm claiming and acting on these words in
Psalm 77:11–14 (ESV), "I will remember the deeds
of the Lord; yes, I will remember your wonders of
old. I will ponder all your work, and meditate on
your mighty deeds. Your way, O God, is holy.
What god is great like our God? You are the God
who works wonders . . ."

PART 4

Enhancements Through a Refined Perspective

Comfortably Numb

IF YOU'VE EVER HAD THE UNFORTUNATE BUT NECESSARY NEED of receiving an intravenous catheter (IV) prior to or following a health concern, I sure hope you had a nurse like Mary or Christie.

Before I received my dream job of stay-at-home Momma, I served patients in an outpatient surgery center. On days when I worked the pre-op side of the operating room, I loved the interaction with my patients. Their demeanors were pre-sleepy drugs and discomfort. We were able to be genuinely vulnerable with one another, because of my patients' nerves, my love of deep feel, and my lack of filter.

A foot-long spindle of Paw Patrol and Disney princess stickers could be found hanging from the wall in front of me as I recorded my assessment and the patient's vital signs. In my periphery, I could often see a stack of charts awaiting review, in preparation for the next day's surgeries. Some days the stacks were mountains and other days were mole hills, but every day presented its own challenges.

Nursing was a team sport. When I was tied up with charting or holding closed the back of a patient's gown to avoid a "full moon" viewing, my coworkers Mary and Christie would come over to help start IVs.

Mary and Christie were two of my dearest friends. These ladies are masterminds of nursing. After getting all their supplies lined up along the bedside, I would hear them explain to the patient, "Now, there's going to be a sting here, sort of like a bee sting." Don't worry. I kept it classy and withheld my smart aleck commentary. Thankfully, Mary and Christie's demeanors are so gentle and hospitable, the patient didn't have time to question if the sting was the size of a honeybee or the giant Wallace bee that is ten times bigger.

Before inserting the twenty-gauge peripheral intravenous catheter, they would first numb the area surrounding the vein with lidocaine, in hopes that it would be the only stick of a needle that the patient would feel. The teensy size of the needle that held the numbing medicine was an unknown gift to each patient.

Following a successful and tiny injection of lidocaine, the patient was in the homestretch for a smooth IV placement.

However, the two-stick approach is an art. Lidocaine insertion can obliterate the vein, which can lead to a lost blood vessel and at worst, a blown vein. If a vein meets its end, not only does that cause more discomfort to the patient, the two-stick method will not have saved you any sticks because the process must start all over again.

But our patients had *the* Mary and *the* Christie. Not only could these ladies give you the most enjoyable IV experience ever, but they could also teach you how to love your family well and cook a mouthwatering venison stew. Mary and Christie were beyond wise and well-versed in how to live well, both within the realm of their scrub-wearing hours and outside the workplace.

Might I add that even the most competent and wise nurses can't numb everything. I've taken a whack at this numbing skill set, both inside and outside of the pre-op area.

As I've endured different levels of heartbreaks and calamities throughout life, I've had to question if a numbing approach is fitting for my situation or if I should *feel* the ripping and stretching of my heart muscles.

I'm definitely a believer in the numbing out process. Or at least I used to be.

As I mentioned in the previous chapter, after my initial hour of shock and crying out for the Lord to save my daddy, realization hit me that my stress level could produce harm in our unborn, high-risk baby.

Having just lost our baby Ruth a year before, I felt raging bile creeping up my throat at the thought of another death.

The only remedy I could conjure up was to anesthetize myself.

No, I didn't drink alcohol or smoke a doobie to detach myself from actuality. I was pregnant, y'all. I wouldn't even eat lunch meat, despite the OK from both of my doctors *and* the Google.

This was beyond lunch meat avoidance. I decided that in order to protect my baby, I had to unleash a self-inflicted, mental and heartful paralysis on myself.

Somehow my mind administered a head-to-toe, long-lasting dose of lidocaine that left me magically yet harmfully numb to the harsh emotions and destruction of my life. It was as if I suddenly had the head nodding powers of Jeannie from the 1960s fantasy sitcom, *I Dream of Jeannie*.

My daddy had a heart attack. Our baby had a heart that was essentially broken and would require major surgery to have any chance of survival outside the womb. Boy, what I would have given to have had a genie bottle that I could have held myself captive in to escape the chaos and agony of my existence.

I had to stop feeling.

I had to stop bawling.

I had to stop thinking, because even if I didn't snort and gasp for air in a full-out cry session, my body and heart were reacting to my subconscious. Remember all the fascinating things we learned through Marsha's trauma story we discussed in the science chapters of this book? The brain is constantly working and reacting. And my body was definitely telling the story of what was happening in my heart and mind.

I ignorantly thought that somehow I could trick my brain and body into not responding to the trauma within me. I convinced myself to somehow try and block nerve receptors in my prefrontal cortex. If my grief went through processing in this region of my brain, out of control hormones and neurochemicals could lead me to fatigue, increased blood pressure, anxiety, difficulty concentrating, irritability and disturbed sleep. And what my body endured, so did that of the little love who was intertwined with me. If my body's responses led to an early arrival for our baby and then, at the very worst, her not surviving because of prematurity on top of her known congenital heart defect, I didn't know how I would live with myself and my cloud of guilt.

There could be none of that.

In the words of one of my daddy's favorite bands, Pink Floyd, I went "comfortably numb." To desensitize myself seemed like the most rational decision in my current, broken perspective. This was me unknowingly and ignorantly digging myself a deeper hole of hurt and trauma that I would have to later try and claw out of. I don't recommend this route on a grief journey. However, if you're reading this and you're already in that deep, dark hole of numbness, I am pleased to report that the God of the impossible will lovingly pull us from the depth and restore our feelings to health. I can vouch for it.

In my cheerleader knockout scenario discussed in earlier chapters, my cheerleader self now lay limp and numb on a bench along the sidelines of life. I watched the lips of people move in everyday interactions, but I couldn't hear what they were saying, much less muster up the brainpower to process the unheard words. My once hyped-up daily self felt drained of all joy. Life had beaten me down and I wasn't helping myself by going numb. I love this quote by a wise and compassionate counselor, Melissa Trevathan: "When you numb the dark, you numb the light. And when we're numb, we lose our joy."[16] I was a numbed out, warm body walking around Arkansas with a smothered joy flame in my soul.

Sadly enough, I know that I have way too much company in this numbing out approach.

Your marriage is so rocky, the feeling of nothing is the most satisfying feeling of all.

The increase in your financial obligations is so towering, to sever the connection of responsibility and self with alcohol is most desirable.

When you wake up with sweat-soaked hair and a racing heart at two in the morning, you realize that the PTSD of childhood trauma or unintentional hurt from today's church is more than you can bear. You would rather live in a life bubble of nothingness and resentment than have to face the grace and forgiveness that should be offered to the guilty party.

We are all prone to trying to deaden the blows of fear and uncertainty, flaky attitudes and false perceptions, unrealistic expectations, and changes that are both pleasant and unpleasant. We're all riding this struggle bus together.

Now, turn on some jiving music or take a walk around the block, because we're about to sit in some truths as we wait for the lidocaine's numbing effects to wear off from our self-induced dulled state. God never ever intended for us to live in such a fog.

In fact, while we're at it, let's go ahead and go bald eagle on the situation.

Check It

1: Do you practice a form of numbing out when life gets hard? How can you break that practice and allow yourself to feel?

2: How's that self-directed neuroplasticity going? You're doing awesome! Keep up with these biblical meditations, prayers, thoughts of thanks, and talking with loved ones about the importance of your perspective each day.

Affirmation (Come on, sister! Say it loud! Say it proud!)

God, you are with me here.

God, you were with me there.

God, you are with me everywhere in my life.

Through the happy and the hurt, *you are with me,*
and you love me without end.

I'm claiming and acting on these words in
Psalm 77:11–14 (ESV), "I will remember the deeds
of the Lord; yes, I will remember your wonders of
old. I will ponder all your work, and meditate on
your mighty deeds. Your way, O God, is holy.
What god is great like our God? You are the God
who works wonders . . ."

Fly Like an Eagle

IRST, CAN WE ADDRESS THE CRAZY PLAY ON WORDS AT hand?

Bald eagle.

In my thirty-plus years of living, I have yet to lay eyes on an eagle that was lacking feathers.

Turns out, there is a very clear-cut explanation of this oxymoron that ends as a paradox. Maybe as I sat in my high school biology class, I was too busy daydreaming about boys or what kind of weekend fun would unfold, but it wasn't until recently that I grasped the meaning behind the name of America's great bird.

Entirely covered with white feathers on their heads and their tails, filled in with dark brown feathers coating them from neck to legs, eagles are quite the opposite of bald.

Their name actually comes from the Old English word *balde*, meaning white.

Aha! White-headed eagle computes perfectly in my brain.

If you had a front-row seat to a bald eagle and any other feathered creature sitting on a limb as a storm rolled in, two different scenes would unfold.

Sparrows, bluebirds, cardinals, and all other feathered friends would seek to find shelter and flee from the rain and storms. The eagle, on the other hand, would head straight into the unsettled weather.

Eagles look for storms. They understand storms. While other birds flee gushing winds and beating rain, eagles find comfort in such conditions. Once the eagle pushes into the storm, he allows the power of the cloudburst to push him higher, allowing his seven-foot wingspan to extend and glide. It is in this gliding on great heights that the eagle finds rest. He no longer has to flap and search. His bravery in facing the force of the storm essentially grants him the freedom to find rest.[17]

Talk about an insightful and heartening visual.

For most of my life, I have been the blue jay, frantically seeking shelter and safety in storms of life. I always signed up for the lidocaine numbing shot when given the opportunity to dodge anguish.

But let me tell you about a prayer I once said that led me to finding myself pushed into the center of the storm. I was forced to put away my blue feathers and suit up in the fashion of my nation's great bird of strength and freedom.

After losing our daughter Ruth and experiencing the Lord move in my life in ways beyond my boxed-in, Bible Belt faith, I asked God to fill me with more of Him and less of me. To rid me of myself and overflow me with His intoxicating love, strength, grace, and joy.

Following my prayer, I found myself confronted with storms of pain, loss, doubt, and anger. My eagle suit was on, and I had to go in.

I had to feel the brutal gusts of wind and hail.

The storms forced me to change as a person.

It was my time to affirm who I believed God to be. We're told, "The one who lives under the protection of the Most High dwells in the shadow of the Almighty. I will say concerning the LORD, who is my refuge and my fortress, my God in whom I trust" (Psalm 91:1–2 CSB). Would I have the courage to stand on those Psalm 91 words, fully trusting God and finding refuge under His wings in my trials and harsh weather moments?

Never had I been so heartfully depleted as when I lost my daddy. We can all recount the circumstances that leave us so bare and downright fuzzy in the brain, can't we? The eagle knows the only way to get past a storm is to fly through it. Robert Frost wrote, "the best way out is always through." Yours truly didn't have the instinct of an eagle or the wisdom of a poet when grief slowly strangled me with a profound grip of destruction following the loss of my daddy. My world and very heartbeat hasn't been the same since 2018.

I hate how true I find these words to be.

My Disney-loving, happy-go-lucky roots fuel me to detour life's foreseen unhappy and hard. Life sure doesn't always bring about the best of feelings. As I rest in the God of my storms I am so comforted by His truths from scripture and the focus on heaven and its purity. God's restoring power and might through the enhancing of my perspective over the past six years has helped me to fully recognize the anxiety and panic that coaxes me to grab my blue jay suit when life starts to feel fragile and too unknown. I'm now able to quickly say no and turn to grab the eagle suit. After entering life's storms and being pushed to heights I would have never reached on my own, I have finally found permission to glide. As I rest in the God of my storms, I am so comforted by His truths from scripture and the focus on heaven and its purity.

You can also rest in the God of your storms. We don't have to numb out. We can feel.

Jesus was the single, perfect human being to have ever set foot on this earth. And the only one who ever will.

Even in His absolute perfectionism, Jesus *felt*. Emotions were not something that He swept under the rug while donning His best poker face.

For instance, in John 2:13–17 we see a big display of Jesus's feelings. One day when Jesus arrived at the temple in Jerusalem, He found people selling animals, making His Father's house a place of trade. He didn't tell the guilty parties to go to detention hall. He also didn't turn His head and walk away in denial.

Jesus went straight into the storm. He drove out all the people and animals. He overturned tables and poured out coins. Jesus held no reserve in displaying His anger and frustration about the situation. He would not stand for such disrespect in His Father's house.

In another example of great emotion, Jesus attended synagogue on the Sabbath. First, let's revisit a rule of the Sabbath. One of the Ten Commandments found in Exodus 20:8–10 (CSB) states, "Remember the Sabbath day, to keep it holy: You are to labor six days and do all your work, but the seventh day is a Sabbath to the LORD your God. You must not do any work—you, your son or daughter, your male or female servant, your livestock, or the resident alien who is within your city gates." Noted.

Now, back to Jesus attending synagogue on the Sabbath. The bracketed additions for clarity here are mine. "Jesus entered the synagogue again, and a man was there who had a shriveled hand. In order to accuse him [Jesus], they [the Pharisees] were watching him closely to see whether he would heal him on the Sabbath. He told the man with the shriveled hand, 'Stand before us.' Then he said to them, 'Is it lawful to do good on the Sabbath or to do evil, to save life or to kill?' But they were silent. After looking around at them with anger, he was grieved at the hardness of their hearts and told the man, 'Stretch out your hand.' So he stretched it out, and his hand was restored. Immediately the Pharisees went out and started plotting with the Herodians against him, how they might kill him [Jesus]" (Mark 3:1–6 CSB).

So short story, Jesus saw a child of God who needed healing. The Pharisees had overanalyzed and reworded God's commandment to not work on the Sabbath, as the Son of God could not heal on the Sabbath because healing was working. *Hm.* That's not what God said. He said don't work. The verse before the reading in Mark 3,

Jesus said "The Sabbath was made for man and not man for the Sabbath. So then, the Son of Man is Lord even of the Sabbath" (2:28–28). Jesus simply clarifies that God gave us the Sabbath as a gift. But the mean old Pharisees wanted Jesus out of the picture. Jesus's truth and light were outshining their warped teachings and leadership, leaving them to look for any excuse to get Him in trouble and have Him killed.

The Bible clearly states that Jesus looked at the Pharisees with anger. He flew into the storm of doubting humans and accusations.

Jesus showed anger. He also grieved the hardness of the Pharisees' hearts. On this day, Jesus defended a man in need with both action and righteous rage. After all, the two greatest commandments from God are to love Him and love His people (Mark 12:30–31). Jesus was doing just that as He brought healing to the man's shriveled hand.

And in the shortest verse of the Bible, John 11:35, we learn "Jesus wept." Those two words provide us with further understanding of Jesus's range of emotions.

If you're like me, it moves you to know that God in the flesh cried and mourned. Even though He knew His friend Lazarus would be raised to life by His own voice, Jesus chose to feel with Mary and Martha the intensity of sorrow upon their brother's death. Jesus didn't numb out and watch their human bodies respond in anguish and questioning. Rather, He joined them in their despair and gave them permission to *feel.*

That permission is exactly what brings peace to this girl's heart! And I hope it will to yours too.

Throughout the Bible, we read over and over that Jesus had compassion on people. I love how the feeling of compassion is of such great importance and emphasis throughout Scripture. Jesus had compassion for the blind, those with leprosy, family members whose loved ones had died, the hungry, the helpless, and the harassed.

This means Jesus has compassion for *us*, my friend. We all fall under the blanket of hurting and weary. Jesus's compassion wasn't a simple Southern, "Well, bless your heart. I'll pray for you." Nah! Jesus was literally moved by the feelings of empathy and concern for the hurting people around him.

Compassion in Greek is the word *splagchnizomai* (say that three times while savoring a slice of spanakopita). And if you're thinking that *splagchnizomai* is the name of a creature that you can find stomping through the woods of Arkansas, though incorrect, I do appreciate your imagination.

Splagchnizomai means to be moved so deeply by something that you feel it in the pit of your stomach.

When Jesus saw the hurt and brokenness of Lazarus's sisters, He felt their sorrow in the pit of His stomach. Though He knew how the story would end with the raising of Lazarus's dead body to life, again, He chose to display human emotion and exemplify the permission to feel deeply in the quake of our lives.

Jesus wasn't half-heartedly connected to mankind. He didn't spend His days as a recluse in a stone structure, in hopes of avoiding the sight of human brokenness around Him.

He didn't just notice our pain, He felt it in the pit of His stomach. He walked dirt roads that were crawling with individuals worn down by various diseases or any number of personal challenges. Jesus sat in boats and waded through the sea waters with anxious and doubt-filled friends.

Y'all, I know we think we're busy and have too much to conquer on our lists and calendar obligations. But if the Son of God, who held all power and carried all the weight of the world on His shoulders could stop. Sit. Listen. And break bread with others. Shouldn't we be able to do the same?

In Matthew 8:23–27, a raging storm brewed while Jesus and His disciples were at sea. The boat was all but capsized. Jesus's disciples were distraught and pleading for the sleeping Savior to rescue them from the storm. After calling out the men on their faith, Jesus spoke and rebuked the winds and the sea. Following the power of His words, there was a great calm. I can picture Jesus's disciples with faces of codfish as they marveled at the miracle that had unfolded right before their eyes. Those same men said, "What sort of man is this, that even winds and sea obey him?" (v. 27 ESV).

I'll chime in on that one.

As I sat in my mom-wagon parked beside my daddy's grave a month after his passing, the sun setting in the west was breathtakingly displayed across the sky. It was a cool summer's evening. No rain. No wind. Just God's masterful art skills painted all around me.

Bethel's song "It Is Well" was blaring over the Bose speakers. Large, salty tears poured over my non-waterproof mascara. It hurt so much to think of saying, "It is well" when *nothing* about my current situation was well. The loss of numb control was involuntary. I had tried to hold it together but there was too much pressure built up within my broken spirit.

I sat very pregnant behind my steering wheel and wrestled with God in my heart and out loud. For believing wholeheartedly in His sovereignty, I sure could play harsh cards of doubt and resentment.

I know I'm such a punk kid. God is so patient and kind to us, y'all. Even in our questioning, He stays right there beside us.

I always love hearing people tell of times they prayed to see Jesus and saw their prayers answered in beautiful ways. Some say they saw Him in their dreams or as they were walking down the road.

I was begging God for one of these encounters of my own.

My faith was teetering.

I needed to know that God was truly present and listening. After all, my prayer asking Him to save my daddy wasn't answered. So I began to doubt His positioning.

I probably cried out for this Jesus sighting for a good two minutes.

Nothing.

Even after focusing in on the bushes and flowers around me with my very best abstract eye, I still couldn't make out an image of Jesus.

Cry-singing along to the lyrics of "It Is Well," something remarkable happened. As the words, "The waves and wind still know His name,"[18] vibrated through the speakers, the American flag that had been hanging lifelessly before my eyes throughout my stay began to blow in the wind.

The flag rippled from the pole a good five times before coming to a standstill again. For the remainder of my cemetery visit, there was no wind.

It wasn't just any random wind. That billowing flag moment was an answered prayer. A gift to my trembling heart. In that faith-resuscitating moment, I realized that God *does* stay with us in the storm. And it took effort from my end to switch my perspective and be open to seeing God in the whispers of the winds and in the words of Scripture.

My grief wasn't over at this point, and not all my prayers were answered in the way that I asked, but I felt such a peace come over me. It was as if I had new breath in my lungs and the stamina to push through the long and unrevealed journey ahead of me in my grief.

Jesus, the same man the disciples marveled about, wondering if the wind and seas would obey Him, is the same man who told the wind to blow and bring a faith boost to my quivering heart.

God allowed me to feel and see His very presence.

Friends, we have to feel.

Let's feel in the times of celebration and achievement, but also in the times of doubt.

If you're not in the middle of a life storm at this moment, be sure to fill up your water bottle and clean your flying goggles, because something is brewing. For some of us, a storm will hit much sooner than later.

As you start to pick up and move forward with pieces of a shattered heart, allow yourself to feel where those fractured bits came from.

Don't lather on the lidocaine or whatever form of "numb out" you choose.

Take flight like the eagle and go into the storm.

Allow the power from within your struggle to lift you up to heights above the storm.

It's there that you will take a breath, stretch your trembling wings, and glide while resting in the God of the storm.

Check It

1: Are you currently in a storm of life? Are you flying into the storm or dodging it altogether? Remember the words of truth and encouragement from Isaiah 40:31: "But those who trust in the LORD will renew their strength; they will soar on wings like eagles; they will run and not become weary, they will walk and not faint" (CSB).

2: Can you recall a moment in time where you asked God for His presence to be very obviously revealed to you? If not, maybe ask Him now and wait patiently in hopeful anticipation of when that revealing will come. Remember to keep your perspective in check during the hours, days, or weeks of waiting.

Affirmation (Come on, sister! Say it loud! Say it proud!)

God, you are with me here.

God, you were with me there.

God, you are with me everywhere in my life.

Through the happy and the hurt, *you are with me,*
and you love me without end.

I'm claiming and acting on these words in
Psalm 77:11–14 (ESV), "I will remember the deeds
of the Lord; yes, I will remember your wonders of
old. I will ponder all your work, and meditate on
your mighty deeds. Your way, O God, is holy.
What god is great like our God? You are the God
who works wonders . . ."

Glamorous Scars

"*A* LOVELY DAY, LOVELY DAY, LOVELY DAY . . ." ECHOED through my iPhone speaker. How could I not wake up to feel lovely with Bill Withers and his joyous tunes?

I'll tell you how.

As I did a quick and slightly blind gaze in the mirror on my passing through to the bathroom, I was unpleasantly surprised to find a natural hazard upon my forehead.

Yikes! Lovely day, my foot. I better get some assistance in hiding this elephant-sized pimple before I frighten the public. As I rummaged through my lime green, waffle-weave makeup bag, I said an inward prayer of thanks for so many instruments of enhancement.

My Goof Proof eyebrow pencil was like a bad habit—once I found it and realized its power over my fumbling makeup-applying hand, I landed myself a user's problem and will not be able to give it up without going through a rigorous rehab program.

My golden tube of concealer was there and ready to save me, again. Its sticker read, "Cover up discoloration, spots, dark circles under eyes, imperfections." Yahtzee.

That's exactly what I needed—assistance in covering up the bulging imperfection above my left eyebrow.

Have you ever looked at yourself in the mirror and started nitpicking what you would call imperfections or flaws?

Sometimes our "mirror" is in the form of another human who verbalizes too much, too often, and in too harsh a tone. A loving child may remind us of our need to schedule a hair appointment as they refer to us as "having skunk lines" on top of our head. A cantankerous grandmother squeezes the extra jiggle where our solid triceps used to reside in high school and says, "You've been eatin' good, haven't you, sugar?" I mean, sure, the truth hurts. But *rude*!

Yet most often I'm my own worst critic. I don't know if I'll ever look at my body and not see it as a life-sized connect-the-dots/freckles game.

Grace, grace. We've got to extend it to ourselves and others. All of those harsh truths of outward features are not flaws. They're human traits. Our society has deemed the Instagram-unfiltered men and women of today as having "imperfections." Commercials, internet ads, and billboards display the most outwardly perfect beings of mankind but they're only so perfect thanks to advanced airbrushing and editing technologies.

I'll be the first to admit I sassed my parents when they would lovingly remind me in my childhood of 1 Samuel 16:7, "Humans do not see what the LORD sees, for humans see what is visible, but the LORD sees the heart" (CSB). Not only would I spout off in a tone that now makes my blood boil when my children use it with me, I would cut my eyes at them when they gifted me with words of affirmations and encouragement. They would call me beautiful, but *beautiful* wasn't even a word within my teenage radar at the time—unless I was wowing over someone else.

Oh, what I would give to go back and grab the shoulders of my fit, ten percent body fat self, and say, "Pull yourself together! You think your parents don't know their head from a hole in the ground, but, sister, you have got it going on—in the physical and heart sense! Stop torturing yourself physically and mentally with comparison. Listen to the wise counsel God has so intentionally placed in your life."

Ah, to be young and a punk. To this day, I'm occasionally found guilty of playing the punk card, but I am *definitely older* now. Currently, I'm trying to figure out how in the world I'm going to graciously handle it when our three daughters regularly dish out that same sassy attitude as their once-teenage mother did. Sheesh.

All sarcasm and laughing aside, my parents were right. God's perspective is truly focused on our heart posture and not a pimple on the face or increasing number on the scales.

We see eyes with what we would call dinky, short lashes that need a *stat* appointment with an esthetician. God sees two eyes that can perceive the world He created and the people in it—if only we'd use our eyes to see ourselves as a reflection of God. And once we clearly see who we are, we can use those eyes to focus on others.

One summer evening, Austin and I found ourselves in a rare form. We were getting ready for a date night. An evening of dressing fancy, curling my hair, and frosting myself with jewelry that is not kid-friendly in its dangle length . . . occasions all far from my daily norm.

Thank goodness for the gracious light bulb wattage in the bathroom and closet. As I unwound my final strand of hair from the wand, I thought, *Girl, you're looking all right, and that makeup is on point tonight*—declarations I seldom believe or speak over myself.

From stage left, in skipped our curly headed twins. Dressed in their favorite PAW Patrol sleepwear, the sisters were revved up and ready to roll in a night of fun with grandparents while Mommy and Daddy hit the town.

After *finally* putting trust into the jeans that were most forgiving of my mom bod, a reality bomb was dropped right there on my closet floor. "Mommy, we don't color on ourselves, only on paper!"

Ah nuts, one of our truth-giving sister-girls had zoned in on my "motherhood marks"—you know, those bands of white lines that tell a story of some type of change and season in our lives. Stretch mark scars.

I could have taken a gentler road for myself and responded as if she were inquiring of my C-section disfigurement, but the honesty bug was biting me hard. Her gleaming eyes were dancing all around that scar.

Don't worry, I contained my back talk and reassured the sisters that I had not colored on my body, but those lines were, in fact, from a season of my life when I carried their sweet selves in my tummy. Those scars defined a season of life when my heart and body were both growing at uncontrollable rates.

Aside from the mushy, heartfelt words, I did thank the girls for reminding me to play my barre workout video and apply lotion more often.

We all have scars, both internal and external, that proclaim a story.

Some scars are subtle while others are incredibly evident and often stand as conversation pieces. Sometimes, scars leave us feeling confident—because that brutal fall we took on the soccer field was the precursor to the winning goal in the game. Maybe our scar shouts of how lucky we were to walk out alive from a car accident—sure, it stretches from our hip to our ankle, and we would go broke trying to cover it daily with concealer. But y'all, we don't have to go there. It's not about the size of the scar as much as it is about the *story* behind it.

In 2018 when Austin and I brought home our thirty-six-day–old Julianna from the hospital for the first time, our family was over the moon to have all five of us sleeping under the same roof. A short fourteen days prior to Julianna's homecoming, her flawlessly smooth-skinned, newborn body had undergone open-heart surgery. Her scar is about four inches long. She also has two smaller scars on her torso and leg from lifesaving tubes doctors had to pierce through her once unblemished skin during her ICU stay.

A few weeks after getting settled into our new norm as a family of five, I was changing Julianna's clothes on our bedroom floor. The master bedroom is typically where you could find the clean laundry. Sure, it should be crisply folded or ironed and tucked away in my people's bedrooms, but it took this momma a hot minute to get back in the groove of non-hospital life.

Atalie bebopped into our bedroom as the lyrics of Mandisa played over the radio. She was wearing her Portland Timbers soccer uniform her daddy had brought home for her and Emmie as a souvenir the summer before.

She plopped down on the floor next to me and said, "Look at Julianna's scar, Mommy! It looks really good!"

I replied, "You're right, baby. J's scar is looking good. Atalie, what is a scar—what does that word mean?"

Atalie rolled over onto her back and mimicked the legs-in-the-air baby stance Julianna was challenging me with during her wardrobe change. Without skipping a beat, she spouted, "It means it's healing!"

And just like that, a then four-year-old rocked my world with her words of wisdom. She was right. A scar is a sign of healing—of new growth.

For years of my life up until this point, I saw scars as misfortune. They were puzzle pieces to hide or cover up.

But on that day, our preschooler enlightened me to the fact that a scar doesn't mean that place is going to look the same as it did before the hurt or injury, *but* there is a newness surfacing.

Let's quickly touch on some more anatomy and physiology wonder, shall we?

Scar tissue is stronger than ordinary skin. Scars are made up of fibers, not skin cells. What looks like a mark of misfortune and possible weakness is actually a symbol of strength!

I could sit in that all day.

We all have diverse scars. Some are very visible, like Julianna's. She will have her "grace mark" for the rest of her life, to remind her of God's healing hand on her life. That scar isn't just there for her, but it's also there for us. There are marks like that in all our lives—sometimes we can only view life through our own struggles, but when we view a scar of someone else's, we begin to grasp and comprehend the depth of pain and experience that earned the fibrous scar tissue.

For some of us, our scars aren't outward in appearance, but they're on our hearts and minds. Even though we can't see them, we can recall those words and situations that hurt us and left that injury within. Sometimes it's the silence from others that inflict injury on us internally, as well. Internal or external, each type of wound sets up shop for the growing of new fibers that will one day reveal healing and strength at the site.

Society is quick to suggest a need for us to hide our scars. It's tempting and readily available to go and buy the cream to help it fade. Why not make the appointment for lasering and injections? Freeze that bad boy off with cryotherapy.

What if our first thought isn't *How can I hide it?* but *How can I share it?* We could intentionally stop and search for the beauty and purpose of the story behind our scar. I daresay we could be confident and thankful for it.

One of my favorite songs is "Scars" by I Am They. The lyrics are an account of how our brokenness and hurts can lead us to understand Jesus's unending peace and tenderness. And when we can't, yet, say thank you for our own scars, we can always be thankful for the nail scarred hands of Jesus. For His love sacrifice.

I couldn't always say thank you for my scars. Not thank you for my heartache or the actual wound, but *thank you for my scars.* Seriously. It took many months, prayers, and wrestling matches with God before I could even clear away the hurtful smudges of reality that covered my life lens.

When we lose our job or loved ones, no matter the circumstances, it's not a normal human response to say, *Oh, thank you, God, for this trial and hole in my heart. Thank you.*

Now, I didn't say that it was impossible. And I'm certainly not saying that we're thankful for the injury that left us with wounds to be scar-filled. We're not thankful for hardship and empty seats at the dinner table. We're just not. When we love deeply, as the Lord loves us, our hurt is as deep as the love of our loved one or situation.

Friends, it has taken me years of questioning and listening at the feet of Jesus, but I can now say *Thank you, God, for my scars*. Not *Thank you for the loss of our babies and the cancer diagnoses* but *Thank you for the healing and growth that formed from my losses*. Through my agony, I grew to know *God's heart* more and more.

S: SOVEREIGN AND SUSTAINING

C: COMPASSIONATE

A: ALIVE AND ACTIVE

R: RESTORATIVE

S: STEADFAST IN LOVE

These are the words that point to who I found our God to be in the makeup of my scar tissue.

If you're like me, you have some tendencies of the disciple, Thomas—I need to *see* it to believe.

Isn't it wild to recall that when Jesus was resurrected from the dead, He came back whole and full of life—*yet with nail-scarred hands*?

Chills. Down. My. Forearms.

My friends, there is purpose in our scars. Let's thank God for the victories and mountaintops of our lives. Let's also thank God for our scars—for the healing, lessons, and deep connection He has provided us in times where we felt defeat and stuck in the valley low.

But I get it—sometimes when we're in the thick of the struggle and the hurt, we can't catch our breath in the waves of the storm. We can't see beyond the endless unknowns that are surrounding us. I'm right there *with you* if you're thinking it's too hard to be thankful for the scars that are to come when the wound is still so fresh and damaged.

Yet in the middle of the healing process when the pain is still present and it can be hard to put together words of thanks, I'm challenging us to *thank Him for His scars.*

It's because of Jesus's scars that we see the ultimate sacrifice made from deep love for us. The resurrection is the foundation of our faith—that's what His scars are there to remind us of!

One of my go-to scriptures is found in John 16:33. It states that we *will* have trouble in this world. Not that we will *possibly* have trouble, we *will.* But in His goodness, Jesus brings us peace in knowing that He has *overcome* this sin- and hurt-filled world.

Just as a Band-Aid provides covering over an injury during the healing process, let the peace of Jesus cover you in times of trouble and heartache. I hope when you see a Band-Aid from now on, you think of John 16:33.

Jesus brings us peace in the mainstream of hurt and healing.

Think back on your own scars—both inward and outward. Recall the story that God has so specifically written for you in those weaving fibers.

Remember how He has **S**ustained you.

Remember His **C**ompassion on you.

Remember how He has been **A**ctive and working in your life.

Remember how He has **R**estored you throughout time.

Remember how His love for you is **S**teady and unwavering.

Does your perspective in this moment look different than it did during the unfolding of the hard and hurtful?

When we fully grasp the freedom given to us through Jesus' scars, we can fully embrace the beauty of who we are because of Whose we are. And from that realization, we can learn to shine spotlights on our scars that are outward and inward; inviting others to embrace their scars and strength within.

Check It

1: Look in the mirror and ask yourself: *Who or what do I see in my reflection?* Are you being judge-y and harsh as you look at yourself without a filter? Or are you truly seeing the *beautiful, one-of-a-kind you* that God so intricately created with love and purpose?

2: What story can you share with others from any outward or inward scars that you have? Remember those fibers of the scar are evidence of strength in you.

Affirmation (Come on, sister! Say it loud! Say it proud!)

God, you are with me here.

God, you were with me there.

God, you are with me everywhere in my life.

Through the happy and the hurt, *you are with me,* and you love me without end.

I'm claiming and acting on these words in Psalm 77:11–14 (ESV), "I will remember the deeds of the Lord; yes, I will remember your wonders of old. I will ponder all your work, and meditate on your mighty deeds. Your way, O God, is holy. What god is great like our God? You are the God who works wonders . . ."

Thankful for the Sun and Jesus

SN'T IT AMAZING HOW THE SLIGHTEST BIT OF LIGHT CAN illuminate a dark room? How many times have you walked through your home in the dark, and as you stumble around, you freeze and find that the moonlight or streetlight outside your window is ever so scantly streaming through the crack in your blinds—and suddenly you can see. Minutes earlier, you extended your hands out in front of you as a white cane—blindly navigating through darkness and hoping to grasp anything for orientation while avoiding bumping into your surroundings. Yet after a mere twenty seconds, that tiny beam of light that is several dozen feet away has allowed you to see paths and objects on your journey through your home.

I'm finding that people's lives either resemble light or darkness. And the words and actions that overflow from our hearts can either help or hinder someone's journey in life. A light-beaming heart can spur lives into a forward motion toward traction and a next step. On the other hand, a heart of darkness can leave us feeling like we're down in a basement room where it takes extra time and effort for a light source to emerge, all the while we feel that we're stuck or continuing to run into things as we fumble around and attempt to navigate our way.

Truth within people equals radiance and *light*. *Secrecy* and *lies* built up within the human heart and mind equal gloom and *darkness*.

We've got to strive to surround ourselves with truth-holding, light-sourcing friends and family members. In the same breath, if we all need the illumination of truth in our day-to-day living, we need to practice what we preach, and be a beacon of truth for those around us as well.

Just as the gleam from the moon or street lamp can penetrate light into our homes and overtake the darkness, so can the truth-telling, graciously lavished love of a Christ follower.

Darkness cannot overcome light. It simply can't.

Light from the sun can reach a depth of around 260 feet in the ocean, which is about the equivalent of a twenty-four-story building. That's a long quest for a sunbeam. If you've ever ventured beyond the waters of the shoreline, then you know how dark it can seem beneath the surface water. Yet our eyes adjust, and the light starts to overtake the dark.

A laboratory professional peers through a microscope to zoom in and assess a blood specimen that lies on the slide below. A light is passed through the machine to magnify the sample and bring clarity and diagnosis of the symptoms you've been enduring for weeks.

When surgeries are performed in the operating room, there are several light sources used during the procedure to better reveal the truth in front of the doctor and surgery staff. Headlamps, scopes, and overhead lights, all provide a better view of the target area and bring guidance for a more successful outcome.

Light cannot be hidden.

Light reaches far and deep.

Light magnifies.

Light is a powerful weapon, and we wield it every day. We need to pause and determine if we are using that weapon to bring truth, grace, and love to those around us.

I have a friend named Natalie who, I'm convinced, must be an angel on earth. In my twenty-plus years of knowing her, she has exuded a sense of joy and optimism that is hard to grasp. How is she always so upbeat and positive, even when she has trials of not-good and downright hard in her life? Her merry perspective continually draws me in and anchors my heart.

Whether I pull up to the drive-thru pharmacy to see her working behind the desk, or I receive a text and see her name appear across my phone screen, I can expect heartfelt words of encouragement, or the most radiant and genuine smile that calms my nerves in an instant.

Maybe you have a Natalie, that you're thinking of from your own friend circle.

In the stress following our youngest daughter Julianna's near-death experience on day two of her life, I found myself quite overwhelmed with reality—and people. It was a mere six hours after I'd been discharged from my hospital and my momma took me to the hospital where Julianna lay so critically ill. Up until this point, Austin had been the one with Julianna at the children's hospital ever since she was born and transferred from my birthing hospital. Once I was physically on the scene with our sick baby girl, I began to experience waves of anxiety like I had never known.

I sat next to our baby in a blue swivel stool with a pounding heart and a racing mind as the sound of beeping hospital machines filled the room. Being separated so much from our twins was breaking what pieces of my heart felt semi-put together. I could have really used a hug and pep talk from my daddy to tell me in his strong embrace and calm a voice that "everything will be OK, kid." But now he was gone and I still hadn't fully accepted that reality. Every fiber in my being longed to hold our Atalie and Emmie—who were at home with friends and family. The game plan on hospital stays was that Austin and I would stay together at the hospital during the day and tag team the night shifts. Yes, this plan worked best given the sorry circumstances, but it was a familiar feeling of us as ships passing in the night that I remembered well from the early months following our twins' birth. With Austin as my person, in high stress moments I need his reassurance and presence more than ever.

On this highly anxious day at the children's hospital, my momma graciously offered to drive me to our house so I could shower and freshen up before returning to, again, sit next to our sedated daughter. I accepted her offer. And upon leaving the hospital I took two pain pills in attempt to ease the twinge of my two-day fresh cesarean incision.

I remember riding a mile away from the hospital and panicking, as I replayed the last thirty minutes of life in my mind and realized that I had taken *two* pain pills, even though the prescription on my bottle read, *Take one pill.*

My daddy had just passed away three months earlier.

We had to put our twelve-year-old dog down a month before Julianna's birth.

Our youngest daughter was breathing by way of a mechanical ventilator machine.

Gloom and worse-case scenarios seemed to be the hand of cards that I was holding in life at the time. Darkness and fear pumped through my veins. I was in dire need of some light and truth of Jesus spoken over me in this moment.

My unintentional taking of an extra pain pill registered as a death from overdose.

In my panic, I reached out to my friend, Natalie, and asked for her professional insight on my current situation. Pharmacist friends are irreplaceable.

"Natalie, I'm freaking out. How bad is it if I just took two 5mg/325mg Percocet when I was only supposed to take one? I took a 600mg Ibuprofen an hour and a half ago—I think."

"Girl, you're totally fine taking two pills. You are completely safe within the dosing range for your weight and health." And then she said, "How are you? Julianna's pictures are just beautiful!" It was one of those moments when Guinness World Record–holder Chris Nikic's dad ran in during an agonizing stretch of Chris's triathlon. With laser focus and spot-on words of encouragement and love, Chris's dad helped him to push through a moment of uncertainty and understand that he was not alone in his endeavors. That's exactly what Natalie did for me in that moment. She has always been a well of truth and grace to draw from.

Had I been in a non-stressed state of mind, I would not have thought twice about taking the two pills rather than one, because in my surgery working days I called in these prescriptions daily for my patients. I was well aware of the prescribing guidelines, and two pills was, indeed, a safe dose.

Stressed, exhausted, fearful, and post-birth-hormonal nutty was the definition beside my name on that day. And many days to follow.

Natalie provided my frantic and quivering heart so much peace. Darkness and lies of fear consumed me from each lingering thought of what was to come in the hours and days ahead. The glimmering light and honesty that Natalie spoke into my current situation completely overtook the darkness and deceit that were suffocating me from within.

I sure hope you have a friend like Natalie. Someone whose very tone of voice can spark hope in you. Even when they tell you a hard truth or talk nitty-gritty, their mind is so eternally focused that every word they say points to the glory of your Creator and leaves you accepting of this broken world while patiently longing for the perfect heaven that God has waiting for His people. I also hope that your friend is so full of mercy they allow you to be as dramatic, pessimistic, and off-your-rocker as you need to be in your moments of terror—and they don't judge you or hold a grudge against you in the weeks to come following your human actions. That's a true friend.

Good news! We can all be a Natalie even if we don't have a Natalie in our lives. We can bring truth and light into the lives of those around us with our words, smiles, actions, or embrace.

In a moment of sheer tizzy, Natalie spoke life into my heart.

She also gave me a plant when we moved into our new house a couple of years after Julianna was born. Which segues us into my next train of thought. Choo! Choo! *(wink, wink)*

In a super-condensed and non-educated photosynthesis rendition, plants use energy from the sunlight to provide us humans with oxygen. Wouldn't that make perfect sense to say that *light literally gives us life.*

Reflecting back on Natalie calming my dismantled state of being in a high-stress moment, the message is because plants had light from the sun, Natalie had oxygen from the plants to breathe and live.

From her pulsating heart and very breath, she provided me with her life-filled, oxygen-rich elements when my fear was depriving me of a crucial viability factor.

Natalie's secret (but not so secret) source of joy and optimism comes from her reverence and relationship with the God who created light in the darkness on His first day of creation. In John 18 Jesus says, "Everyone who is of the truth listens to my voice." (v. 37, CSB). Natalie's ears are fervently tuned in to the voice of Jesus.

In Micah 7:8, a guy named Micah said, ". . . though I sit in darkness, the LORD will be my light" (CSB). There's a picture of hope and radiance for our dark and weary souls!

That same God who provided Micah with light in the darkness is the light source within Natalie that drives her to encourage and love others so well.

Plants do a lot of cool things for us, but the One who spoke those plants into existence, is the ultimate Light and Life of the world.

Jesus Christ is Natalie's source of light, and from that life-giving connection is opportunity for her to pour light and life into those around her.

To survive and thrive in this world where the darkness of lies, cruelty, and pride *try* to overtake the light of honesty, kindness, and humility, we will forever require a saving light source.

We need the light of Jesus.

When our elder neighbor is struggling to pull her post-Christmas overflowing trash can to the curb, we have the choice to turn our tired selves around and walk back into our garage and act like we never saw anything, or we can spark life and goodness into her soul as we offer to help get the can to the curb.

We each have the choice to be lifegiving people of truth and love to the world around us.

On the flip side of the coin, we have the choice to play into darkness—our choices can add layers of lies, hurt, deceit, and pain on others' if we do not choose our words and actions wisely.

One of the most eye-opening and challenging Sunday school lessons I ever walked through was reviewing and unwinding the tough sayings of Jesus.

First and foremost, I was at a point in my faith journey where I was still under the impression that the word *Jesus* and all His lessons equaled words that were good, pure, and hunky-dory. That is, until my eyes zoomed in on a few verses from Matthew 10:34–39, which tells us Jesus didn't come to bring peace to the world, but a sword.

Wait, say *what*? That sure sounds unloving and dangerous. I'm pretty sure my left ear tilted to my shoulder, like a dog tilts its head as to say *huh*?

Yep. It's there. The not-so-joyful words of Jesus not coming to bring peace. Now remember, we can't just pick one or two verses from the Bible (or any written work), and pull them from their context, so let's look further into the verses that follow. It states that household members will be enemies. Family members will turn against each other.

Ouch. I sure didn't like that or believe it for a minute.

Yet here I am years later, and my aha moment has arrived.

A sword has two sides. In my mental picture, Jesus brings a sword that has two sides—and it's up to us which side of the sword we will stand on.

Satan loves to destroy families and relationships. When he comes at us with a sword, he truly wants to bring trauma and pain, because he's twisted and mean like that. His dividing is out of sheer hate, jealousy, and torment.

Satan is darkness. He's malicious. His intentions in this world are to steal, kill, and destroy just like we read in John 10:10.

Satan wants to steal relationships from us.

Satan wants to kill marriages and create a domino effect of chaos and scarring that will affect all our friends and family members for decades following the injured relationship.

Satan wants to destroy our very source of joy and drive to live an upstanding and wholesome life.

And those are just a few examples of the outcomes that the Enemy desires to achieve from his vile nature.

When scripture tells us that Jesus will bring a sword, Jesus is not intentionally driving a fence between us and our loved ones. It's our call as to which side of the sword we will be on. Will we be on the side of truth and light? Or will we be on the side of lies and darkness?

In this sin-filled world, families are going to stand on opposite sides of the sword. Affairs, theft, gluttony, beat-down self-esteem, lies, and everyday beliefs will cause us to stand on one side or the other, whether we realize it or not.

If you wonder why family gatherings or friend circles are so awkward, you might step back and consider the beliefs and events of each person's life. When you connect the dots, you'll probably start to find patterns and proof of who mingles well with whom.

Jesus brings light and truth. Satan brings darkness, secrecy, and lies.

Hang on. Here is a kicker. Jesus tells us to pray for our enemies.

Wah wah wah.

"But I tell you, love your enemies and pray for those who persecute you" (Matthew 5:44 CSB). There we have it. One of the greatest challenges for me in my faith journey. I love grace extended to me, but it sure can be unnerving to extend it to others. Especially when they've hurt me and my people. Aren't we all this way?

Sometimes I want to proclaim that it is beyond my human capabilities to love and pray for my enemies. But it's not. That particular command stomps on my toes. It takes a lot of heart work and perspective checking on my part to get to the point that I want to forgive and pray for those who have inflicted division and hurt into mine and my family's lives. Humanly, I just want to write them off and not waste my breath or brain space on them.

But God. God calls us to love *and* forgive.

It's hard stuff to think and talk about, y'all. I get it. You're not alone when you want to punch some folks in the face for their poor choices and wrong doings. Sometimes it's myself that needs a quick knock to the noggin.

Please know that this Arkansas girl is over here analyzing her own heart too. God will provide us the strength and grace to do the right thing—but we must work with Him. We've got to choose to reveal truth and life to others. When our perspective is gospel-centered, we won't stray so easily from the road of doing what is right—even when it's the hard thing to do.

If you're a follower of Jesus, you've probably realized by now that Jesus didn't promise for our lives to be painted daily with rainbows and sunshine.

It's the opposite. A life that is actively pursuing and following Jesus should prepare for turbulence and storms.

Satan is going to try to knock us off course. He shrieks in gladness when darkness and lies shake us to the core.

Pssshh—Satan is such a sore loser. Jesus has already defeated death. Therefore, Satan is powerless. *He has no hold over you or me.* Let's claim it!

We *must* focus on our own perspective in the day to day and not allow the broken light sources of others to distract and affect our lives.

According to Isaac Newton, a band of visible colors like red, orange, yellow, green, blue, and purple, appear when a slight beam of sunlight hits a glass prism on an angle. That's a science-y fun fact.

But what if we look at the trials of our lives as the glass prisms. When the light and truth of Jesus hits our prism of battles and despair within our hearts, bands of beautiful colors can be created. God can make rainbows from our trials.

Isn't that beautiful? Don't we all crave to see beauty and amazement brought from our hurts in life?

I've mentioned that one of Julianna's very best friends is the daughter of one of her heart surgeons—her daddy is one of the brilliant surgeons who physically touched our baby girl's heart in the operating room on that September surgery day. Through God's kindness in the gift of their friendship, I see rainbows when Julianna and her friend hold hands and share granola bars at the dance studio each week—despite the itchy and uncomfortable feels that pulsate through my veins when my mind rewinds to our painstakingly difficult days in the CVICU years ago. Their very friendship is a powerful light source in my heart.

If we walk with Jesus, the Light of the World, we will not walk in darkness, but will have the light of life.

I've always surrendered to the complexity of physics. Yet the purpose and power of light within that field of study is amazing to me.

A rainbow of glory to God can illuminate from our trials if we allow biblical truths to pierce through us.

Light can't be hidden.

Light reaches far.

Light magnifies.

We as humans can be light sources like Natalie who spur on and help bring life and truth to those around us.

Go let it shine, sister!

Check It

1: Who serves as a great beacon of light and truth in your life? Are you serving as a light and truth-giver to those around you?

2: Can you think of a time in your life when God brought rainbows and good from a season that was once hard and gray?

Affirmation (Come on, sister! Say it loud! Say it proud!)

God, you are with me here.

God, you were with me there.

God, you are with me everywhere in my life.

Through the happy and the hurt, *you are with me,*
and you love me without end.

I'm claiming and acting on these words in
Psalm 77:11–14 (ESV), "I will remember the deeds

of the Lord; yes, I will remember your wonders of old. I will ponder all your work, and meditate on your mighty deeds. Your way, O God, is holy. What god is great like our God? You are the God who works wonders . . ."

Aha! I See!

It was a vibrant May morning when my honey and I ventured up a mountain that reached more than one thousand feet above sea level.

That may not sound like a great feat if you're a regular alpinist, but please remember the 100 percent humidity that we endure in conjunction with triple-digit Arkansas temperatures.

Cut your girl some slack here. That range of mountain definitely presented some unpleasant sensations as Austin and I scurried to the summit.

Austin could have easily run the whole way to the top with *maybe* two stops to hyperoxygenate his lungs. On my eighth stop to breathe and check for a pulse, I waved for him to keep going. I "smiled" as a fit-as-fit-can-be mom wearing a two-year-old on her back passed me at my pit stop.

Austin also smiled at the toddler-wearing-lady as he turned back around to check on me. I'm certain that his smile wasn't nearly as forced as mine.

"Don't worry, I'll catch up. You keep going," I sputtered. I knew full well that if he went on, chances are I would have never made it to the top.

"No, baby, we're getting to the top of this thing to-gether. I'm not leaving you behind. Come on. You got this. We're almost there. We're just taking a step at a time."

As much as I needed these life-giving words to reach the top of a mountain, don't we all need to hear these words from loved ones when we're trying to reach a finish line to a healthier us, more strict finances, or rehab?

Austin refused to leave me alone. He could have mo-seyed on up the mountain, but he chose to stay with me. He spoke words of encouragement to me, rather than belittling my climbing abilities. Turns out he's as ruthless on the side of a mountain as he is on a soccer field.

On the journey up I saw the house of some family friends. We once stood on their back patio looking at the mountain on July Fourth while eating hot dogs and exchanging fun and laughter. From their patio, the pinnacle that we were aiming to reach looked brutally intimidating. The pitch of the mountain is what makes for a strained body on the way up. But when you're walking the trail up to the pinnacle you don't see it in its entirety, so you don't grasp the intensity of incline at that level.

As I stood (breathing and alive, I might add) on the slope of this beastly piece of nature, our friend's home looked so tiny. And I assure you that their four thou-sand–plus square foot house is anything but tiny.

Again, things aren't always what they seem. It's all a matter of perspective from our lens of viewing.

Austin and I certainly didn't break any records for reaching the pinnacle on that May morning, thanks to my fourteen stops both ways. But we did make it to the top. And you better believe we took multiple pictures to document this incredible feat that I wasn't sure would happen or not.

The beauty of the river and landform around us was absolutely breathtaking. It was a moment of beholding that I will forever cherish. On this day that we were celebrating our wedding anniversary by scaling the mountain hand in hand, a zoomed-out life lesson from thirty-thousand feet was revealed.

This mountain escapade of ours is a lot like the journey of life, right?

We have a goal and a vision of what direction we're headed in.

As we embark on the journey, our adrenaline is pumping and our Little Engine "I think I can, I think I can" voice rings loud and clear. We get the promotion at work. We graduate college and have a stellar job lined up. Our savings account feels really cush. Holiday gatherings are packed out with no open seats.

But as we encounter the pressure changes and unforeseen shifts of terrain, our confidence tanks start to run on fumes. We don't get the promotion at work. We graduate college but have had zero interview calls from the thirty-plus applications we have submitted. A health issue arises and begins to deplete our once cushy-feeling savings account. Loved ones pass away and empty seats at holiday gatherings leave us with pulsating pressure in our chests and a joy flame in our hearts that is fighting hard to stay lit.

If we don't have friends and family championing us with words of authenticity and love throughout our life journey, we'll either find ourselves throwing in the towel and heading back down the mountain without reaching our goal, or we'll push ourselves to limits with empty tanks that eventually leave us stalled and broken on the path. Either way, it's a flop on reaching our goals and joy-filled states.

Between the influence that we surround ourselves with, and our own drive within, we must find that balance of truth and grace.

Sometimes we need to turn the dial back on the truth in a moment that is desperate and dependent on more grace. Other times, we need to crank up the dial of truth and put on our big people underwear because hard-to-swallow-truth is exactly what we need to hear in order to pick ourselves up and continue on our life's journey.

The key to adapting to life's happenings is by using a dial and not a breaker box. Though we can often feel simply on or off in our daily encounters, we need to acclimate and control the resistance we allow in life's triumphs and trials. With a biblical perspective as our guiding compass, we are way more likely to kindly and graciously dial up or down in our reactions and words.

For too long, my perspective was too far focused on all the negatives and not dialed in enough to the good around me. You know that saying that talks about when one door closes, another opens? Sure, I've heard it all my life but in times of deep trials I find myself stuck in front of and beating my hands on the closed door, while mindfully and eyeballingly dismissing the awareness of the two hallways with open doors a few steps over.

It's hard.

It is painstakingly difficult to take our eyes off the closed door of happiness that we knew for so long. Please don't hear me say that we can follow through with this advice and just instantly go from sad and focused on sad, to happy and focused on happy at the drop of a hat. That creates an open slate for a mental health diagnosis.

Thankfully, God has equiped us with everything we need to be able to slowly continue walking down the hall of our life where we will find new doors open, and we'll be shockingly surprised to find that they, too, can bring happiness.

God's word and the affirming truth-telling words of others are our crutches as we hobble down our life's hallway, dismantled and depleted. But how powerful are those words that others give to rally us on? How impactful are the words we use to cheer on others in their hobbling?

Super powerful.

Hellen Keller was an American educator, author, and advocate for the deaf and blind. When she was a little over a year and a half old, Helen developed a febrile illness that left her deaf and blind. She knew very well the challenges of not hearing or seeing. Her teacher, Anne Sullivan, taught her that, "The best and most beautiful things in the world cannot be seen or even touched, but just felt in the heart."[19] I love that. And I believe that Anne Sullivan hit the nail on the head because the Holy Spirit cannot be seen or touched but only felt in the heart. The constant presence of God is all around us. Isn't that the best and most beautiful thing for us to possess?

Check It

1: List your top three goals in this season of your life. Maybe they're relational, physical, spiritual, financial, or something else. Now, who is journeying with you up the mountain of life to pull you up on the days that you feel like quitting?

2: Having one of those no-good-very-bad-Eeyore kind of days? I got you. Joshua 1:9 says, "Be strong and courageous. Do not be frightened, and do not be dismayed, for the LORD your God is with you wherever you go" (ESV). *God is with you wherever you go.* All the way to the finish lines of the goals or sitting at a rest stop while you try to catch a breath and regroup. You are never alone.

Affirmation (Come on, sister! Say it loud! Say it proud!)

God, you are with me here.

God, you were with me there.

God, you are with me everywhere in my life.

Through the happy and the hurt, *you are with me,*
and you love me without end.

I'm claiming and acting on these words in
Psalm 77:11–14 (ESV), "I will remember the deeds
of the Lord; yes, I will remember your wonders of
old. I will ponder all your work, and meditate on
your mighty deeds. Your way, O God, is holy.
What god is great like our God? You are the God
who works wonders . . ."

Honey, Yes You Can

FRIENDS, I SURE HOPE THAT THIS JOURNEY OF SELF-directed neuroplasticity and revealing of heartfelt happies and struggles has helped to simmer your anxiety and refill your heart tank as much as it has mine. I love that we serve a God so big and mighty and full of faithfulness that He hasn't given up on His children—on us.

I once heard a sermon that unfolded the presence of God in a powerful way. Let me take a whack at repeating parts of it. When God created Adam and Eve in the Garden of Eden, He was physically present with them. In Genesis 3:8 there is reference of Adam and Eve hearing the sound of the Lord walking in the garden. And even after Adam and Eve sinned and had to leave the perfection of a world that God created for His children, He didn't stop loving them. God's presence with His people between this time in the garden and Jesus's birth could be seen through fire, water, cloud, the Ark of the Covenant, or the tabernacle. Once Emmanuel, God with us, was born into this world, men and women could see the physical presence of God again. Jesus was God in the flesh. John 1:14 says, "The Word became flesh and dwelt among us. We observed his glory, the glory as the one and only Son from the Father, full of grace and truth" (CSB). Jesus, the scripture that was revealed in human form, walked dirt roads with people. He broke bread and ate meals with friends. He saw and reached out to the least of these. As we've discussed, Jesus didn't just hang out in complete solitude away from all the sin-filled mankind around Him. He chose to sit with the broken-hearted, the betrayed, the stinky, and the contagious. And through His living, He exemplified for you and me how we are to live. Hebrews 4:15 (CSB) reminds us, "For we do not have a high priest who is unable to sympathize with our weaknesses, but one who has been tempted in every way as we are, yet without sin." Remember, Jesus gave us permission to feel. We can see that in the story of His life on earth. As Jesus's time on earth came to a close, God again continued to make a way and remain present with His people. John chapters 16 through 18 reinforce how important it would be for the Holy Spirit to come. Jesus said in John 14:26 (ESV), "But the Helper, the Holy Spirit, whom the Father will send in my name, he will teach you all things and bring to your *remembrance* all that I have said to you" (emphasis mine). There's that word remember that is so key in the exercises that we've been doing at the end of each chapter! And so, God's presence is now with us through the Holy Spirit.

A path to eternity with God in heaven, a place of absolute perfection and zero heartache, is the offer on the table to us from God. It doesn't take a bunch of fancy, well-rehearsed words to ask God to be the boss of our lives. It's quite simple. He just wants our humble words that ask for forgiveness and proclaim our need for Him as our Savior. There's no need for big vocabulary words. And once we reside in heaven after life in this temporary world, God will be with us *still*. He is so good to give us the words in scripture to promise us that His presence will continue to be with us in the eternal world. Listen to this proof in Revelation: "Then I heard a loud voice from the throne: Look, *God's dwelling is with humanity*, and *he will live with them*. They will be his peoples, and *God himself will be with them* and will be their God. He will wipe away every tear from their eyes. Death will be no more; grief, crying, and pain will be no more, because the previous things have passed away" (Revelation 21:3–4 CSB; emphasis mine). Yes. Yes. And Amen! I am clinging to these verses. The thought of such perfection and happiness just seems unreal. Yet science, nature, creation, and the medical world seem pretty unreal too—and because I have seen God's faithfulness and hand in those realms, I haven't a doubt that a remarkable and unreal heaven will be exactly as He says it will.

Y'all, we were designed to be in God's presence. We've always been and always will be His "for you I will." From the beginning of time and until eternity, God has been and will be with us. He wanted it that way. And even when we sin and feel like giving up in this life, He jumps into our lane with open arms and continues to encourage us to finish our earthly lives strong. I can often feel these bottomless desires in my heart for constant joy, zero confrontation with other humans, and a physical body that is flawless and without a glitch. Ha! I've yet to find an app, social group, book, or a bank account that can fulfill these deep desires. So I've wrestled it out and settled it within myself and I've come to the conclusion and acceptance that I was made for another world—and heaven is that world. Turns out, this perfectness that I want so badly is exactly what God wants for you and me. Starting with Adam and Eve getting to live in flawless dreaminess in the Garden of Eden at the beginning of time. That same perfection is what we're guaranteed to enjoy with our Creator in heaven once our time is up on this flip-flopped, temporary earth. When we get to that perfect world that we were made for—the one that fulfills all of our deepest desires—we will celebrate, praise, and bask in the goodness of God. And we'll do all of those fun and happy things with Him right by our side. However, while we're here on earth we get to walk through our struggles and heartaches *with* God. How's that for a flip of perspective? Right now on earth is our only time to *suffer* and *hurt with* God alongside us, because once we're in the perfection of heaven, there's no more suffering and hurt for us to experience! OK! Yes ma'am! Happy heaven is waiting for us. Until we get there, let's use every breath and ounce of energy to love others well, bring glory to our Savior, and tussle through the trying times arm-locked with God.

Whew. That was a lot of unpacking *from* my heart *to* yours. What a journey to a renewed perspective.

Let's continue to hinge together on the fact that *we can't plan our circumstances in life, but we can plan our perspective on how we live through those circumstances*. We worked on building that planned perspective throughout this book and *you nailed it*! Was it easy? Nope. Was it quick? I don't know, how fast do you read? I'm being silly. It's actually a daily teasing process to keep our perspective in check. Is it a pain-free and feel-good process? *Psh*, please. But, honey, it was 100 percent possible, right?

As we press rewind to the reel of our lives and intentionally view it all through the lens of God's unwavering presence with us, we can still see some scraggly threads in our life sock, but we're seeing them in a new light. Lo and behold, as we pull on that thread and zoom in on where it is, we start to discover beauty in the mess.

One of my daddy's key phrases in life was, "Life's not always fun, kid, but the sun will come up tomorrow." I'm holding tight to this verbiage. If we turn on the news or read a billboard as we're driving down the road, we can easily gain a self-constructed perspective of pride, fear, or entitlement. The highlights of our society are often narrative prompts for "life stinks and the world will likely end tomorrow." Thankfully we have the narrative of *hope* from Jesus's spoken truth in John16:33 that in this world we will have trouble, but not to worry because He has overcome the world. Every day since our babies and my momma and daddy went to heaven, the sun has continued to emerge. Even on cloudy days, there is a light beam that overtakes the dreary sky.

Though years have passed, each time our children reach new milestones and accomplishments in their lives, I want nothing more than to call and tell their Yaya and Pappy about the brilliance of their grandchildren. I want so badly for our girls to be able to receive the calls of "Good luck!" and "Great job!" and "I just wanted to tell you that I love you" that their Yaya and Pappy always dialed in to my phone for them. In these sucker punch reality moments, I can still find myself at the feet of God wanting to step into a wrestling match over how unfair it feels that they are no longer here on earth. Do you, also, stand outside the wrestling mat, pulling on the ring and being self-aware that you might be one hurt away from jumping into a match with God? You're not alone in that. But let's intentionally remember and focus on God's presence, sovereignty, and glory to be revealed through our times of hurt.

When people do or say hurtful things to me and my people, my mouth so quickly wants to run without stopping to breathe and process first. It's in these want-to-jaw moments that I soak in the mantra that my momma taught me to live out: "In a world where you can be anything, be kind." The pulsating in my ears from heightened blood pressure in those dramatic moments lets me know that *being kind* sounds much easier when you read it on paper than when you live out those encounters in life. Yet it's the narrow and right way. That being kind phrase falls under the arch of Matthew 22, where we learn that the two greatest commandments are to love God and to love His people. The not-so-trafficked roads of kindness, love, inclusion, and forgiveness are what get us to the finish lines of loving God and loving people well. Let's ride these narrow roads together!

Hopefully you've experienced some positive self-directed neuroplasticity throughout our journey (*wink, wink*). We've continuously confirmed God's presence with us and remembered that He is the same God on the good and yuck days of our lives. The more we use that pathway in our brain, those claims and beliefs become second nature and easier to use. When the struggles with marriage, fertility, parenting, grief, or heartbreak from any catastrophe arise, we've given ourselves a well-paved mental pathway of truth and love to continuously reel through.

Let's be persistent in using our thoughts and words for love, building others up, truth-telling, grace-extending, forgiveness, and good. We don't need millions of dollars to extend kindness and goodness to others. Our level of education doesn't effect our kindness muscle either. What we do need is a chosen filter or perspective that ripples out good for God's people and glory for Him! Remember, we're not doing all of this by our own strength and ability but by the joy of the Lord!

And from a girl who has never been the same since the turning of all the events in my life that I've shared with you, I wouldn't want to go back to the me before the hurts. This Lauren the Lamenter is really starting to grow on me.

I've concluded that cheerleaders bring constant pep and community. They don't just show up to the games where the odds are stacked in their team's favor. And they don't up and leave when the team is getting stomped on by their opponent. They show up, stay, and support. I think I'll keep my megaphone and cheerleader title after all.

Psalm 119:71 (CSB) says, "It was good for me to be afflicted so that I could learn your statues." Jennifer Rothschild, an endearing teacher of God's word who so delightfully balances playful and mesmerizing as she helps others to understand and relate to scripture, helped give me some insight to the word *affliction* that Psalm 119:71 refers to. She said, "What the psalmist calls 'affliction' we could call 'trials' or a million other things that go wrong in our lives. But God can use affliction as a form of loving resistence to keep us from going astray or to guide us back to His Word. Sister, don't resent God if He resists you. Often, what feels like resistance is an affirmation that you belong to Him."[20]

I 100 percent agree that in my days of groaning, questioning, and brokenness, God has deeply affirmed to me that I am His child and am loved so big. That sounds so weird to say but the truth sets us free, right? On the other side of all my struggles I've felt and seen God's presence like never before. It has been so freeing (and at times scary) to fully grasp the fact that I have zero control over my life or the lives of my loved ones. I've learned to be more intentional of being where my feet are and not taking even the smallest joys for granted. I'm feeling all the feels as I've learned and leaned into the truth of Jesus being a King that endured the same emotions. Daily I'm challenged by the verse in John 3 that says, "He must increase, but I must decrease" (v. 30 CSB). I'm running after the God who made us in His image—and in His days on earth a man of sorrow Himself. I don't want to just be like Jesus on the has-it-all-together days, I want to be like Him on the messy, heartbreaking, and frustrating ones, as well. Will you join me in that?

Let's say this affirmation *together* one last time.

God you are with me here.

God you were with me there.

God you are with me everywhere in my life.

Through the happy and the hurt, *you are with me,* and *you love me* without end. I'm claiming and acting on these words in Psalm 77:11–14 (ESV), "I will remember the deeds of the Lord; yes, I will remember your wonders of old. I will ponder all your work, and meditate on your mighty deeds. Your way, O God, is holy. What god is great like our God? You are the God who works wonders . . ."

Yahoo! It's time for us to get out there in the world and do this thing called life—and do it well. Let's daily check our perspective through a lens of love, strength, truth, community, and remembering. *We can* forever lean fully into a gracious and thankful perspective. Oh, honey, yes we can!

Friends, I'm going to close us out with a prayer for you:

I pray that you have the strength to get through this day with enough left over to give some to a neighbor. I pray that you have eyes to see the truth and the words to communicate it. I pray that God will give you quick recall and clarity in remembering all the ways that He has worked wonders throughout your life—even in the teensiest moments. I pray that you find community wherever you are, and that you understand the ways to contribute to it. I pray you find the well of peace and a way to refill it when you need more. I pray that your perspective allows you to see the way, the truth, and the life for every day. God, we love you. We need You. We trust You. We thank You. And we praise You. It's in your mighty Son Jesus's name that we pray. Amen.

A Note from Lauren

FRIENDS,

My sincerest *thank you* for reading this book. Every time I reworked a sentence, trembled behind the keyboard with tear-filled eyes of emotion, or considered throwing in the towel on this unveiling of my deepest hurts and helps, I was thinking of you. I couldn't shake the thought of having so much life-giving hope, love, and wisdom extended to me so graciously by God and His people and then just keeping it to myself. (That would be rude.) I know the comfort and hope that fuels my heart when I hear stories from others who have felt and thought the same wonky ways as me. Boy, do I pray that you walk away with a camaraderie vibe and a gift of hope after finishing this book, receiving affirmations that you are never ever alone in your anxieties, thoughts, heartaches, victories, or questions. Don't let Satan or the crazy world we live in skew your hard-earned and freshly paved perspective. You've been breaking a mental sweat to pave and continuously travel these rewired neuropathways in your mind! And, honey, *you* did it! You have put in the hard work as you intentionally and consistently pondered and affirmed truth and life at the end of each chapter. I'm throwing lots of high fives your way.

You are loved, seen, and treasured by the Creator of this universe and so many others. When you're having a heavy and off day and the world tries to tell you otherwise, just remember your girl here in Arkansas who is always in your corner. I'm cheering loud and proud for *you*.

Much love,

Lauren ☺

Acknowledgments

THOUGH THE HEARTBEAT OF THIS BOOK IS TO POINT TO GOD, the Author of our lives, I must add that He has placed some exceptional people throughout this book's pages—whether in print or in the undercurrent of encouragement that helped push me to continued obedience in highlighting some of God's wonders.

To my forever love, Austin, this book is just as much yours as it is mine. For fifteen years we have been *one*—in reaching our goals, in the kitchen, in our parenting, in our loving of God's people, and now in this book. It's because of your spoken encouragement, insight, and humor that these words have been able to conglomerate into a tangible object. Thank you for asking me to marry you on that July day in 2007. And most certainly for continuing to love me with grace, faithfulness, and fun. I love you forever!

To my sister girls, Emmie, Atalie, and Julianna—we did it! I hope you know that you are so much more to this book than just part of the words on the pages. You and your daddy were a pulse within me to finish it strong so that our family can point others to the good and faithful God that we serve. You and Daddy created the space for me to sit with God and work through big faith wonderings. Thank you for your grace in my absences from soccer practices or after-school sidewalk chalking on my writing days. Your chocolate deliveries, smiles, and laughter while I was sitting in front of the computer served as fuel within me. Thank you for believing in me, extending grace, giving big hugs, and understanding that in life, we may have to miss out on some of the momentary fun in order to follow in obedience to Christ—and that obedience will forever pave a road of goodness and more fun ahead. I love you, sisters! You and Daddy are my whole world.

To my Momma and Daddy, the impact of your presence and teachings while in this world serve as the foundational strength for me to be able to move forward with passion, love, and goals each day as you are physically absent. I hope that I can instill a deep love and worthiness into our Emmie, Atalie, and Julianna—just like you did for me and Melissa. Though I will never be the same Lauren as I was when I had you here on earth, I will forever strive to make you proud and stand for what is good, honest, and kind—just as you taught me. I never earned any awards for being a grammar whiz or a queen of the etiquette book. I've always been more likely to bud wings and fly, than to correctly label a compound-complex sentence, yet you continued to encourage me in my passion of words—and drive me to English tutoring. Thank you for believing in me. I will love you forever.

To Bob and Maria Goff, I will always be your hype girl and ready to serve as campaign manager should you ever decide to run for president of our great country . . . or of Disney World. The way you wholeheartedly welcome and empower others with your words and presence is remarkable. Thank you for pouring yes-you-can gasoline onto my heart's desire to write. I can't wait to see the jewels in your crowns once we all go party in heaven! You are indeed a sage of this time! Austin, the girlies, and I love you lots.

To Kimberly Stuart, you'll always be the big sister that I never had. You have the perfect balance of keeping it fun and accomplishing business. After working with you for months and getting to absorb your knowledge of both your heart and mind, I must say that I am *sorry* for my earliest writing submissions. I read back over them with eyebrows raised and a turned-up nose—yet you always met me with a smile and highlights of the parts that were decent wording. A medal for Most Gracious Writing Coach is headed north to you. You are a gem of a writing coach but more than that you are a shining mentor in loving God and loving others well. Thank you for letting me join you in this life of authorship and for loving me and my family despite the random overall appearances and muumuu deliveries. We love you so big!

To my editor and friend, Jamie Chavez, there are no bounds to the ways that I have learned from you. From the get-go, you lovingly took me under wing with all my wacky words and squirrel-chasing thoughts—and from your wise critiquing, I have never felt belittled or unworthy of authorship; you've only encouraged me to stay in my creative space and take the time to process and produce. World's Most Patient Lady medal is headed your way. And though we had just begun the deep dive into the editing of this book when I told you about my momma's cancer diagnosis, you fervently prayed for us and told me to take all the time I needed to be a daughter and caregiver. Your grace and friendship at this point of the editing process taught me more than all the correcting of grammar and sentence structuring combined—and that's *a lot*! Thank you for taking on a project with this stay-at-home-momma from Arkansas. Dunkin' Donuts will always serve as a reminder to me, Austin, and the girlies of how thankful we are for you and the way that God intersected our lives.

To my friends Shelley, Meshali, Kale, Aamie, and Jefe, who endorsed this book, you deserve a standing ovation from me—and you know I'm doing all the embarrassing whoopin' and hollerin' as I stand. Because you know and understand my hyped self, I love you even more for standing behind me on these words of a journey that taught my beat down cheerleader within that I can indeed stay in the game of life because God is with me throughout. You are each a shining star in my world! Lots of love from your girl here in Arkansas!

To my friend and track-changes-coach, Sarah, you are a lifesaver in many ways. Though you endlessly pour out for the pediatric population by day and serve your family 24–7, you stayed up late on a weeknight to teach my overwhelmed-by-track-changes brain how to hide all the red edits so I could see straight and understand what was happening on the computer screen in front of my face. Your kindness to teach me and constantly cheer for me throughout my writing process (and all of life's unfoldings) serves as wind beneath my wings. I'm incredibly thankful that God made us framily and that we get to do this hard and happy life together!

To my girl Natalie—you are a rock. Every text or piece of happy mail that you send is a reminder to me of how kind and loving our God is. You exemplify His goodness on all the levels, and I love you big!

To my friends, family, and hometown of El Dorado, so much of my perspective chiseling comes from getting to do life with you. Thank you for teaching me, loving me, providing me with words to keep going, and remaining a safe place for me to return to.

To my readers—my friends, you are so precious to me. Even though I don't know each of you by name, you were wrapped around my heart as I poured out words through my keyboard. You were who I saw sitting across the table from me as we came together to just be humans with real world happies and hurts. We had any and all barriers down. We poured out tears and all the feels. We laughed until our cheeks hurt. And through it all, we provided one another with the reassurance that we are never alone. You will always be my people.

End Notes

1. Amy Davison, Hillary Morgan Ferrer, "The Impact of Marriage and Divorce on Children: A Conversation with Katy Faust," Mama Bear Apologetics, podcast audio, 13 February 2023, mamabearapologetics.com/82-the-impact-of-marriage-and-divorce-on-children-a-conversation-with-katy-faust (accessed 18 October 2023).

2. Sissy Goff, *The Worry-Free Parent: Living In Confidence So Your Kids Can Too* (Minneapolis, MN: Bethany House, 2023), 21–22.

3. David Eagleman, *Livewired: The Inside Story of the Ever-Changing Brain* (New York: Pantheon Books, 2020).

4. David Eagleman, *Livewired*.

5. Joseph A. Annibali, *Reclaiming Your Brain: How to Calm Your Thoughts, Heal Your Mind, and Bring Your Life Back Under Control* (New York: Avery, 2015), 44–45.

6. Bessel Van Der Kolk, *The Body Keeps the Score: Brain, Mind, and Body in the Healing of Trauma* (New York: Penguin Books, 2015).

7. "Anxiety Disorders – Facts and Statistics," Anxiety and Depression Association of America, adaa.org/understanding-anxiety/facts-statistics (accessed 19 October 2023).

8. Van Der Kolk, *The Body Keeps the Score*.

9. Van der Kolk, *The Body Keeps the Score*.

10. Van der Kolk, *The Body Keeps the Score*.

11. "Dictionary Definition," *Merriam-Webster*, merriam-webster.com/dictionary/altruistic (accessed 20 October 2023).

12. "Anyway: The Paradoxical Commandments," paradoxicalcommandments.com (accessed November 6, 2023).

13. Katherine and Jay Wolf, *Suffer Strong: How to Survive Anything by Redefining Everything* (Grand Rapids, MI: Zondervan, 2020).

14. "About Brandon," Brandon Burlsworth Foundation, brandonburlsworth.org (accessed 20 October 2023).

15. "17 Hours: Chris Nikic's Ironman Story," ESPN, 21 March 2021, youtube.com/watch?v=XsqI-BD2GMs (accessed 27 May 2023).

16. "Getting Your Joy Back," Daystar Counseling Ministries, 2021, vimeo.com/648649841 (accessed 22 October 2023).

17. Patricia Holbrook, "Learn From the Eagle: The Challenger of the Storms," *The Atlanta Journal-Constitution*, 1 August 2019, ajc.com/lifestyles/religion/learn-from-the-eagle-the-challenger-the-storms/juRFhn9zZveJKZEWv2muRI (accessed 22 October 2023).

18. "It Is Well," written by Kristene DiMarco, © 2013 Bethel Music Publishing (ASCAP).

19. Helen Keller quoting Anne Sullivan, *The Story of My Life* (NY: Grosset & Dunlap, 1905), 203.

20. CSB *Lifeway Women's Bible* (Nashville: Holman Bible Publishers, 2022).

About the Author

Lauren lives with her husband, three daughters, and dog in the wilds of Arkansas. This is her first book. You can find her on Instagram, Facebook, and Substack.

www.ingramcontent.com/pod-product-compliance
Lightning Source LLC
Chambersburg PA
CBHW030427160726
47991CB00005B/1623